I Remember Mama

A Play in Two Acts

John Van Druten

A SAMUEL FRENCH ACTING EDITION

SAMUEL FRENCH

FOUNDED 1830

SAMUELFRENCH-LONDON.CO.UK
SAMUELFRENCH.COM

ISBN 978-0-573-01197-9

www.samuelfrench-london.co.uk

www.samuelfrench.com

FOR AMATEUR PRODUCTION ENQUIRIES

UNITED KINGDOM AND WORLD
EXCLUDING NORTH AMERICA
plays@SamuelFrench-London.co.uk
020 7255 4302/01

Each title is subject to availability from Samuel French,

depending upon country of performance.

I REMEMBER MAMA

Produced at the Aldwych Theatre, London, 1948, with the following cast of characters:
(*in the order of their appearance*)

Katrin Hanson	Helen Backlin
Mama	Mady Christians
Papa	Gerard Heinz
Dagmar Hanson	Maureen Davis
Christine Hanson	Henryetta Edwards
Mr Hyde	Maurice Jones
Nels Hanson	Gunnar Hafsten
Aunt Trina	Adrienne Gessner
Aunt Jenny	Lily Kann
Aunt Sigrid	Amy Frank
Uncle Chris	Frederick Valk
A woman	Josephine Dent
Dr Johnson	Daniel King
Mr Thorkelson	Milo Sperber
A Nurse	Pamela Stocks
A Charwoman	Margaret Evans
A Doctor	Peter Grieswood
An Orderly	Vivian Cornell
Elevator Boy	Fred Marshall
Arne	David Cole
Another Nurse	Ethel Ramsay
Soda Clerk	Peter Bartlett
Madeline	Gillian Raine
Dorothy Schiller	Sylvia Clarke
Florence Dana Moorehead	Josephine Wray
Bell-Boy	Peter Bartlett

The play directed by Mady Christians, based on the New York Production by John van Druten

SYNOPSIS OF SCENES

The action of the play takes place in and around the kitchen of a house on Steiner Street, San Francisco, in 1910

NOTE: The stage directions in this script are based on the method of presentation used in the production at the Music Box Theatre, New York. It is possible that these could be simplified or altered in the case of other productions if it should be found necessary.

I REMEMBER MAMA

I Remember Mama is not an easy play for amateurs. Its physical production, at any rate if it is intended to try to duplicate the New York method of presentation, demands facilities infrequently met with in amateur theatres. Revolving stages, platforms, backdrops, traveller curtains and the like are things to discourage even the hardiest group if it has no more than what may be called "standard equipment".

Yet, in preparing this edition, it has seemed to me that the play does offer, by very reason of its difficulties, a challenge and an opportunity to those groups who are more interested in creating something new and in overcoming problems than they are in reproducing the simple one- or two-set plays from the meticulous stage directions printed in the average acting editions. A director of imagination and invention may find in *I Remember Mama* a stimulus to his talents by the need to find a way to put this piece upon his stage, if it appeals to him.

There is always more than one way of staging any play. When I wrote *I Remember Mama* I was fortunate enough to be in the service of a generous and enthusiastic management who were prepared to give me almost anything I asked for. The result was a lavish and beautiful physical production. Yet I remember well the day when our first "run through" was given for the benefit of a few friends. It was played without scenery or furniture other than the usual rehearsal chairs and tables, without the platforms and curtains that are so important a part of the stage show, and naturally without lights or black-outs. Yet the small invited audience was as much moved and enthusiastic as later audiences in the theatre have been. I am aware that this is not wholly a trustworthy sign; our audience that day was composed largely of theatre people whose imaginations were trained to visualize a stage setting from a brief description by the director, and trained, too, to make professional allowances in a way that the average member of a lay audience could not do. But at least that experience does suggest that the text has a quality of appeal that is independent of its method of staging.

Having myself devised the New York production, it is hard for me now to imagine other ways of presenting the play. That is, I think, in any case, the task of each individual director. But there are a few indications that I might helpfully give. The play is devised for alternate scenes— the shorter ones being played down front, and the longer ones on the main stage—rather in the manner of a musical play or of the modern productions of Shakespeare. In New York, the front scenes were played on two small revolving stages or turntables, L and R. These revolves are not essential if some other way can be devised of bringing on and off the actors and the very simple bits of furniture and properties. (The furniture *must* be cleared to give an uninterrupted view of the main

stage, unless perhaps the theatre is equipped with an apron stage of
considerable width, in which case they might be stylised and permanent.)
Possibly this can be done with black-outs for the actors, the furniture
being set and changed by the stagehands in view of the audience, as was
done by the stage-managers on the occasion of the run-through.

The traveller curtains concealing the main stage seem to me to be
essential to enable the changes to be made from kitchen to hospital and
back again, and from the kitchen to Uncle Chris's ranch. I do not think
that the length of the play (it is very long) will permit these changes,
however simplified, to be made in view of the audience; the front or side
scenes must follow instantaneously. But here again an inventive director
may be able to devise a way. The steps which raise the main stage are
not essential, although the variety of levels obtained from their use adds
greatly to the pictorial effect in arrangement of groups. For example,
Mama, standing higher than the aunts when she reads Uncle Chris's
notebook, is much more effective than she would be, standing on the
flat.

The cat will, I think, prove less of a problem than is anticipated. Our
own New York Uncle Elizabeth, adopted from a foundling hospital,
was made to attend every rehearsal, which it spent in the arms of Dagmar
or being led around the stage on a leash, to accustom it to its surroundings;
it was well fed just before each performance, and gave surprisingly little
trouble. From the one occasion when it disappeared (before its under-
study was engaged) I can vouch for the fact that the resurrection scene
loses all point if played with a stuffed cat.

The automobile is a problem because of space and sight-line. Other-
wise it can be hauled on and off on a rope pulled by stagehands, with
the noises being made by separate machinery in the wings. If stage (or
offstage) space is limited, it is possible to dispense with the car altogether
and to rely only on the noises. In this case, Jessie must quite obviously
be shown to the audience walking up and down (she did so even in New
York, for the benefit of those sitting too far over to be able to see the
car), having presumably got out of the car to stretch her legs. She must
be visible before the aunts make their entrance, and may well be seen,
helping Nels with the box of oranges.

These are a few hints only as to the possible handling of problems.
The one thing that cannot be dispensed with is an efficient switchboard.
There are over a hundred light cues in the New York production, and
these and the black-outs are essential (or so it seems to me) to the effec-
tiveness of the show. As I have said, the play is not an easy one, and
should be undertaken only by groups ambitious and interested enough
to give time, thought and imagination to the production. But from the
reception which it has met with in its long New York run I am encouraged
to believe that its appeal is not due to its staging but rather to a basic
reality and humanity in Miss Kathryn Forbes's characters whom it was
my pleasure and privilege to present on the stage.

JOHN VAN DRUTEN

I REMEMBER MAMA*

ACT I

The main scene is the kitchen of the house on Steiner Street, San Francisco, in 1910

Down-stage, on either side, there are small turntables on which the shorter front scenes are played against very simplified backgrounds. As each scene finishes the Lights dim and the table revolves out, leaving an unobstructed view of the main stage. The main stage is raised by two steps, above which running TABS *open and close. (See the Ground Plan at the end of the play)*

When the CURTAIN *rises, Katrin, in a spotlight, is seated at a desk on the* **1** *R turntable, facing the audience. She is writing and smoking a cigarette. Katrin is somewhere in her early twenties. She should be played by an actress who is small in stature, and capable of looking sufficiently a child not to break the illusion in subsequent scenes. She is a blonde. Her hair, when we see her first, is in a modern "up" style, capable of being easily loosened to fall to shoulder length for the childhood scenes. She wears a very short dress, the skirt of which is concealed for the prologue by the desk behind which she is seated. Katrin writes in silence for a few moments, then puts down her pen, takes up her manuscript, and begins to read aloud what she has written.*

Katrin (*reading*) "For as long as I could remember, the house on Steiner Street had been home. Papa and Mama had both been born in Norway, but they came to San Francisco because Mama's sisters were here. All of us were born here. Nels, the oldest and the only boy—my sister Christine—and the littlest sister, Dagmar." (*She puts down her manuscript and looks out front*) It's funny, but when I look back, I always see Nels and Christine and myself looking almost as we do today. I guess that's because the people you see all the time stay the same age in your head. Dagmar's different. She was always the baby—so I see her as a baby. Even Mama—it's funny, but I always see Mama as around forty. She couldn't always have been forty. (*She puts out her cigarette, picks up her manuscript and starts to read again*) "Besides us, there was our boarder, Mr Hyde. Mr Hyde was an Englishman who had once been an actor, and Mama was very impressed by his flowery talk and courtly manners. He used to read aloud to us in the evenings. Bur first and foremost, I remember Mama."

The Light dims down, leaving Katrin only faintly visible

Lights come up on the main stage, revealing the house on Steiner Street— **2** *a kitchen room. There is a dresser up* C, *filled with china. On either side*

---

*N.B. Paragraph 3 on page ii of this Acting Edition regarding photocopying and video-recording should be carefully read.

of the dresser is a door, the one to the R *leads to the pantry, the one to the* L *to the rest of the house. The* L *wall is a short one. It is the wall of the house, and contains a door upstage leading into the street, being presumably the back door of the house, but the one most commonly used as the entry-door. Beyond it the street is visible, with a single lamp-post* L, *just outside the house. Behind the room rises the house itself with upper windows lighted, and behind it a painted backdrop of the San Francisco hills, houses and telegraph posts. The furniture of the kitchen is simple. A table* C, *with two chairs above it, armchairs at either end, and a low bench below it. Against the* R *wall upstage is a large stove, below it another armchair. The window is below the door in the* L *wall and has a low Norwegian chest under it*

"I remember that every Saturday night Mama would sit down by the kitchen table and count out the money Papa had brought home in the little envelope."

By now the tableau is revealed in full, and the Light on Katrin dwindles further. The picture is as she described. Mama—looking around forty—is in the armchair R *of the table, emptying the envelope of its silver dollars and smaller coins. Papa—looking a little older than Mama—stands above her. His English throughout is better than hers, with less accent*

Mama You call the children, Lars. Is good they should know about money.

Papa goes to the door up L, *and calls*

Papa Children! Nels—Christine—Katrin!
Children's Voices (*off; answering*) Coming, Papa!
Mama You call loud for Katrin. She is in her study, maybe.
Papa She is where?
Mama Katrin make the old attic under the roof into a study.
Papa (*amused*) So? (*Shouting*) Katrin! Katrin!
Katrin (*still at her desk*) Yes, Papa. I heard.
Papa (*returning to the room*) A study now, huh? What does Katrin study?
Mama I think Katrin wants to be author.
Papa (*sitting in the armchair* L *of the table*) Author?
Mama Stories she will write. For the magazines. And books, too, maybe, one day.
Papa (*taking out his pipe*) Is good pay to be author?
Mama I don't know. For magazines, I think maybe yes. For books, I think no.
Papa Then she become writer for magazines.
Mama Maybe. But I like she writes books. Like the ones Mr Hyde reads us.

Dagmar enters up R. *She is a plump child of about eight. She carries a cat in her arms*

Dagmar, you bring that cat in again?
Dagmar Sure, she's my Elizabeth—my beautiful Elizabeth! (*She crosses to the chest under the window, and sits, nursing the cat*)

Papa Poor Elizabeth looks as if she had been in fight again.
Dagmar Not poor Elizabeth. *Brave* Elizabeth. Elizabeth's a Viking cat. She fights for her honour!
Papa (*exchanging an amused glance with Mama*) And just what is a cat's honour, little one?
Dagmar The honour of being the bravest cat in San Francisco.

Christine enters up L. *She, like Katrin, should be played by a small young actress, but not a child. Her hair is to her shoulders—her dress short—her age indeterminate. Actually, she is about thirteen at this time. She is the cool, aloof, matter-of-fact one of the family. She carries a box of crayons, scissors and a picture-book*

Aren't you, Elizabeth?
Christine (*sitting* L *above the table and starting to colour the picture-book with the crayons*) That disgusting cat!
Dagmar She's not disgusting. She's beautiful. Beautiful as the dawn!
Christine And when have *you* ever seen the dawn?
Dagmar I haven't seen it, but Mr Hyde read to us about it.

My Hyde enters up L. *He is a slightly seedy, long-haired man in his fifties. Rather of the old-fashioned English "laddie" actor type. He wears a very shabby long overcoat, with a deplorable fur collar, and carries his hat. His accent is English*

Didn't you, Mr Hyde? Didn't you read to us about the dawn?
Mr Hyde (*coming down to Dagmar*) I did, my child of joy. The dawn, the rosy-finger-tipped Aurora . . .
Dagmar When can I get to *see* the dawn, Mama?
Mama Any morning you get up early.
Dagmar Is there a dawn every morning?
Mama Sure.
Dagmar (*incredulously*) It's all that beautiful, and it happens every *morning*? Why didn't anyone *tell* me?
Mr Hyde My child, that is what the poets are for. To tell you of *all* the beautiful things that are happening every day, and that no-one sees until they tell them. (*He starts for the door* L)
Mama You go out, Mr Hyde?
Mr Hyde For a few moments only, dear madam. To buy myself a modicum of that tawny weed, tobacco, that I lust after, as Ben Jonson says. I shall be back in time for our nightly reading.

He goes out L *and disappears down the street, into the wings, off* L

Mama (*rising and going to the door up* L; *calling with a good deal of sharpness and firmness*) Nels! Katrin! You do not hear Papa call you?
Nels (*off*) Coming, Mama!
Katrin (*at her desk*) Yes, Mama. I'm coming.

She rises. In her few moments in the dark, she has loosened her hair to

her shoulders, and we see that her skirt is short as she walks from her desk, and up the steps into the kitchen. As soon as she has left it, the turntable revolves out. Immediately after her, Nels enters up L. He is a tall, strapping young fellow—old enough to look eighteen or nineteen, or fifteen or sixteen, according to his dress or demeanour. Now he is about fifteen

(*To Christine*) Move over. (*She shares Christine's chair at the table with her, sitting R of Christine*)

Papa So now all are here.
Mama Come, then.

Nels sits R above the table. Dagmar remains crooning to Elizabeth, but rises and stands behind Papa

(*Sorting coins*) First, for the landlord.

She makes a pile of silver dollars. It gets pushed down the table from one member of the family to the next, each speaking as he passes it. Papa comes last

Nels (*passing it on*) For the landlord.
Katrin (*doing likewise*) For the landlord.
Christine (*passing it to Papa*) The landlord.
Papa For the landlord. (*He dumps the pile at his end of the table, writing on a piece of paper, which he wraps around the pile*)
Mama (*pushing forward another pile*) For the grocer.

The business is repeated. During this repeat, Dagmar's crooning to the cat becomes audible, contrapuntally to the repetitions of "For the grocer"

Dagmar (*in a crescendo*) In all the United States no cat was as brave as Elizabeth. (*Fortissimo*) In all the *world* no cat was as brave as Elizabeth!
Mama (*gently*) Hush, Dagmar. Quietly. You put Elizabeth back into the pantry.
Dagmar (*in a loud stage whisper, as she crosses to the door up R*) In Heaven or HELL, no cat was as brave as Elizabeth!

She goes out with the cat

Mama For Katrin's shoes to be half-soled. (*She passes a half dollar*)
Nels Katrin's shoes.
Katrin (*proudly*) My shoes!
Christine (*contemptuously*) Katrin's old shoes.
Papa Katrin's shoes.
Christine (*rising and coming R of Mama*) Mama, Teacher says this week I'll need a new notebook.
Mama How much it will be?
Christine A dime.
Mama (*giving her a dime*) For the notebook. You don't lose it.
Christine I won't lose it. (*She wraps it in her handkerchief*)
Mama You take care when you blow your nose.

Christine I'll take care. (*She returns to her seat*)
Papa Is all, Mama?
Mama Is all for this week. Is good. We do not have to go to the bank. (*She starts to gather up the few remaining coins*)

Katrin rises, comes down stage and sits on the steps

Nels (*rising*) Mama . . .

Mama looks up, catching an urgency in Nel's tone. Papa stops smoking for a moment

Mama, I'll be graduating from grammar school next month. Could I— could I go on to High, do you think?
Mama (*pleased*) You want to go to High School?
Nels I'd like to—if you think I could.
Mama Is good.

Papa nods approvingly

Nels (*awkwardly*) It . . . it'll cost a little money. I've got it all written down. (*He produces a piece of paper from his pocket*) Car fare, clothes, notebooks, things I'll really need. I figured it out with Cy Nichols. He went to High last year.

Papa rises and moves behind Mama to look at the paper Nels puts before them

Mama Get the *little* bank, Christine.

Christine rises and gets a small box from the dresser. She brings it to Mama and then sits again. Mama counts the contents

Katrin (*herself again, in the present—looking out front*) The little bank! That was the most important thing in the whole house. It was a box we used to keep for emergencies—like the time when Dagmar had croup and Papa had to go and get medicine to put in the steam kettle. I can *smell* that medicine now! The things that came out of the little bank! Mama was always going to buy herself a warm coat out of it, when there was enough, only there never was.
Nels (*anxiously*) Is there enough, Mama?
Mama (*shaking her head*) Is not much in the little bank right now. We give to the dentist, you remember? And for your roller-skates?
Nels (*his face falling*) I know. And there's your warm coat you've been saving for.
Mama The coat I can get another time. But even so . . . (*She shakes her head*)
Christine You mean Nels can't go to High?
Mama Is not enough here. We do not want to have to go to the bank, do we?
Nels No, Mama, no. I'll work in Dillon's grocery after school.

Mama writes a figure on the paper and starts to count on her fingers. Papa looks over, and does the sum in his head

Papa Is not enough.

Mama (*finishing on her fingers against her collarbone*) No, is not enough.

Papa (*taking his pipe out of his mouth and looking at it a long time*) I give up tobacco.

Mama looks at him, almost speaks, then just touches his sleeve, writes another figure and starts on her fingers again

Christine I'll mind the Maxwell children Friday nights. Katrin can help me.

Mama writes another figure. Papa looks over and calculates again. He nods with satisfaction

Mama (*triumphantly*) Is good! Is enough!

Nels Gee! (*He moves beside Papa down* R *and starts to play with a wire puzzle*)

Mama We do not have to go to the bank. (*She rises, takes the small box to the dresser, then crosses to the stove*)

Dagmar enters up R *without the cat*

Dagmar (*hearing the last line*) Where is the bank?

Christine (*leaving the table, moving down* L, *cutting out the picture which she has coloured*) Downtown.

Dagmar What's it look like?

Christine Just a building.

Dagmar (*sitting on the bench, below the table*) Like a prison?

Christine (*sharply*) No, nothing like a prison.

Dagmar Well, then, why does Mama always say "We don't want to go to the bank"?

Christine Because—well, because no-one ever wants to go to the bank.

Dagmar Why not?

Christine Because if we went to the bank all the time, there'd be no money left there. And then if we couldn't pay our rent, they'd turn us out like Mrs Jensen down the street.

Dagmar You mean, it's like saving some of your candy for tomorrow?

Mama (*busy with coffee and cups at the stove and the dresser*) Yes, my Dagmar. Is exactly like saving your candy.

Dagmar But if—if all the other people go to the bank, then there won't be any money left for us, either.

Nels (*kindly*) It isn't like that, Dagmar. Everyone can only get so much.

Dagmar How much?

Nels However much you've got there—put away. You see, it's *our* money that we put there, to keep safe.

Dagmar When did we put it there?

Nels I—I don't know when. A long time back, I guess. Wasn't it, Mama?

Mama Is enough about the bank.

Dagmar How much money have we got in the bank?

Nels I don't know. How much, Mama?

Mama Enough.

During the last speeches Aunt Trina appears from the wings down L. *She is a timid, mouselike little woman of about forty, with some prettiness about her. She wears her hat and coat, and a pathetic feather boa. She comes up the street and knocks on the house door*

Was the door?

Christine (*moving quickly towards the door up* L) If it's the aunts, I'm going to my boodwar.

Katrin (*rising, entering the scene*) And I'm going to my study.

Mama (*stopping them*) You cannot run away. We must be polite to the aunts. (*She crosses and opens the door* L) Why, is Trina!

Papa Trina, and all by herself!

Mama Say good evening to Aunt Trina, children.

Children (*together*) Good evening, Aunt Trina.

Trina Good evening, children. How well they all look. (*She comes above the table* L)

Mama (*following Trina*) You have a feather boa. Is new. (*Inspecting it*) Beautiful.

Trina (*simpering a little*) It was a present.

Mama (*smiling*) A present! Look, Lars. Trina has a present.

Papa (*moving to Trina and feeling the boa*) Is fine. (*He puts Trina's hat, coat and boa on the chest under the window*)

Mama Jenny and Sigrid don't come with you, Trina?

Trina (*embarrassed*) No, I—I didn't tell them I was coming. I want to talk to you, Marta.

Mama (*smiling*) So? Sit then, and we talk. (*She puts her in Papa's chair,* L *of the table*)

Papa crosses above the table

Trina (*nervously agitated*) Could we talk alone?

Mama Alone?

Trina If you wouldn't mind.

Mama Children, you leave us alone a little. I call you. Dagmar, you go with Katrin.

Katrin (*protesting*) Oh, but Mama . . .

Mama (*firmly*) Katrin, you take Dagmar!

Katrin Yes, Mama. (*Pushing Dagmar, resentfully*) Come on.

Katrin, Dagmar, Christine and Nels go out up L

Mama Now—what is it, Trina?

Trina (*looking down, embarrassed*) Marta . . .

Mama (*helpfully*) Yes?

Trina Oh, no, I can't say it.

Mama (*anxiously*) Trina, what is it?

Trina It's—something very personal.

Mama You want Lars should go outside?

Trina Would you mind, Lars? Just for a minute?

Papa (*good-humouredly*) No, I go. I know what women's secrets are.
(*Teasing*) As your Uncle Chris say—"Vomen! Pff!"
Mama You have your pipe, Lars? Is fine night.

Papa takes out his pipe, then lays it down

What is it?
Papa I forget. I give up tobacco.
Mama Is still some tobacco in your pouch?

Papa nods

Then you do not give up tobacco till you have finish. You give up *more*
tobacco—not the tobacco you already have.
Papa Is not right, Marta.

He pats her, takes his pipe, and goes out L, *outside the house, under the
lamp-post, and stands looking up at the stars, smoking*

Mama (*moving* R *of the table*) So, Trina. Now. What is it?
Trina (L *of the table*) Marta   I want to get married. (*She rises*)
Mama You mean—you want to get married, or there is someone you
want to marry?
Trina (*coming below the table*) There's someone I want to marry.
Mama Does *he* want to marry *you*?
Trina (*sitting on the bench*) He says he does.
Mama (*delighted; moving below the table*) Trina! Is wonderful! (*She sits
beside her*)
Trina (*crying a little*) I think it is.
Mama Who is?
Trina Mr Thorkelson.
Mama From the funeral parlour?

Trina nods. Mama nods, speculatively, but with less enthusiasm

Trina I know he isn't very handsome or—tall. I know it isn't what most
people would think a very nice profession, but . . .
Mama You love him, Trina?

Trina nods ecstatically

Then is good. (*She pats Trina's hand*)
Trina Marta, will you—will you help me tell the others?
Mama Oh—Jenny and Sigrid—they do not know?
Trina No. I was afraid they'd laugh at me. But if *you* tell them . . .
Mama Jenny will not like you tell me first.
Trina (*desperately*) I can't help that. You've got to tell them not to laugh
at me. If they laugh at me, I'll—I'll kill myself.
Mama (*with decision*) Jenny and Sigrid will not laugh. I promise you,
Trina.
Trina Oh, thank you, Marta. And—Uncle Chris?
Mama (*with some seriousness*) Ah!
Trina Will you talk to him?

Mama It is Mr Thorkelson who must talk to Uncle Chris. Always it is the husband who must talk to the head of the family.
Trina Yes. I know, but—well, Uncle Chris is so very frightening. He's so big and black, and he shouts so. And Mr Thorkelson is—(*she gestures a very small man*)—well, kind of timid, really.
Mama (*gently*) But Trina, if he is to be your husband, he must learn not to be timid. You do not want husband should be timid. *You* are timid. It not good when *both* are timid. (*Then firmly*) No! Jenny and Sigrid I speak to, but Mr Thorkelson must go to Uncle Chris.

Papa enters L

Papa Marta, Trina, I do not want to interrupt your talk, but Jenny and Sigrid are coming.
Trina (*alarmed*) Oh, dear! (*She rises quickly*)
Papa I see them get off the cable-car. They come up the hill. (*He crosses above the table*)

Mama rises. She moves round the R *end of the table and above it*

Trina (*in a flurry*) I'd better go to your room for a minute.

She starts for the door up L, *turns back, gets her things from the chest, and runs out, carrying them. Meanwhile, Mama has been whispering the news to Papa*

Mama The coffee is ready—I get more cups. (*She moves up to the dresser, collects five cups and brings them down to the table*)

During the above, Aunts Jenny and Sigrid have entered from the wings down L. *Jenny is a domineering woman in her fifties; Sigrid, whining and complaining*

Sigrid (*in the street*) Wait, Jenny, I must get my breath. This hill kills me every time I climb it.
Jenny You climbed bigger hills than that in the old country.
Sigrid I was a *girl* in the old country.
They march to the door and knock—Sigrid following Jenny

Mama (*opening the door to them*) Jenny. Sigrid. Is surprise. (*To Sigrid*) Where's Ole?
Sigrid Working. He's always working. I never see anything of him at all.
Mama (*crossing to the stove for the coffee-pot*) Is good to work.
Sigrid It's good to see your husband once in a while, too. (*She sits above the table* L)
Jenny (*no nonsense about her*) Has Trina been here? (*She comes* L *of the table*)
Mama (R *of the table*) Trina?
Jenny She's gone somewhere. And she doesn't know anyone but *you* . . .
Mama That is what *you* think.

Jenny What do you mean by that?
Mama Give Lars your coat. I give you some coffee. Then we talk about Trina.

Papa takes Jenny's and Sigrid's coats and puts them on the chest

Sigrid She *has* been here?
Mama (*pouring coffee and passing cups*) Yes, she has been here.
Jenny What did Trina want?
Mama She want to talk to me.
Jenny What about?
Mama Marriage.
Sigrid What?
Mama (*pouring calmly*) *Marriage.* (*She passes Sigrid's cup*) Trina wants to get married.
Jenny (*seated* L *of the table*) That's no news. Of course she wants to get married. Every old maid wants to get married. (*She rolls up her veil*)
Mama There is someone who wants to marry Trina.
Jenny Who'd want to marry Trina?
Mama Mr Thorkelson.
Sigrid Peter Thorkelson? Little Peter? (*She gestures a midget*)
Mama He is not so little.
Sigrid He's hardly bigger than my Arne—and Arne is not ten yet.
Mama So he is hardly bigger than your Arne. Does every husband have to be big man?
Jenny Trina's making it up. That happens with old maids when they get to Trina's age.
Mama (*firmly*) No, Jenny—it is true. Mr Thorkelson wants to marry Trina.
Jenny (*changing her tactics slightly*) Mr Thorkelson. She'd be the laughing stock. (*She laughs, rises and moves* L)
Mama (*moving to Jenny*) Jenny, Trina is here. She will come in in a minute. This is serious for her. You will not laugh at her.
Jenny I shall do what I please.
Mama No, Jenny, you will not.
Jenny And why won't I?
Mama Because I will not let you.
Jenny And how will you stop me?
Mama If you laugh at Trina, I will tell her of the time before your wedding when your husband try to run away.
Sigrid (*rising, intrigued*) What is that?
Jenny Who told you that?
Mama I know.
Sigrid (*intrigued; stealing around and below the table*) Erik—tried to run away?
Jenny It's not true.
Mama Then you do not mind if I tell Trina.
Jenny Uncle Chris told you.
Sigrid (*tenaciously*) Tried to run away?
Mama It does not matter, Sigrid. Jenny will not laugh at Trina now. Nor

will you! For if *you* laugh at her, I will tell her of your wedding night with Ole, when you cry all the time, and he send you back to Mother.

Papa (*with sudden enjoyment*) This I do *not* know!

Mama (*reprovingly*) Is no need you should know. I do not tell these stories for spite—only so they do not laugh at Trina. Call her, Lars. You like more coffee, Jenny? Sigrid?

Papa goes to the door up L

Papa (*calling*) Trina.

Mr Hyde reappears down L, *and lets himself into the house. The Aunts are standing in line with Mama*

Mr Hyde (*seeing company*) Oh, I beg your pardon. I was not aware . . .

Mama Mr Hyde, these are my sisters.

Mr Hyde Enchanted, ladies, madame, madame. The Three Graces.

He bows. Sigrid giggles coyly. Mr Hyde goes to the door up L

You will excuse me?

Mama Sure, Mr Hyde.

Mr Hyde I shall be in my room.

He goes out

Jenny (*moving* L *of the table*) So *that's* your famous boarder. Has he paid you his rent yet? Three months he's been here, hasn't he?

Mama (R *of the table*) Is hard to ask. Surely he will pay soon.

Jenny (*with a snort*) Surely he won't! If I ran my boarding house the way you run this place . . .

Papa Maybe your boarders wouldn't always leave you.

Jenny If Marta thinks she's going to get the warm coat she's always talking about out of *that* one . . .

Mama Jenny, Mr Hyde is a gentleman. He reads to us aloud. Wonderful books—Longfellow, and Charles Dickens, and Fennimore Kipling.

Trina steals in up L. *She hesitates in the doorway*

Come in, Trina. The coffee is getting cold. (*She pours a cup. There is a silence*) I tell them.

Jenny (*to Trina*) Why did you come to Marta first?

Trina comes down to R *of Papa*

Papa She thought Marta would understand.

Jenny Aren't Sigrid and I married women, too?

Papa You have been married longer than Marta. She think maybe you forget.

Trina comes down below the table

Jenny What sort of a living does Mr Thorkelson make?

Trina (*sitting on the bench below the table*) I—I haven't asked.
Sigrid (*sitting* R *of the table*) Can he keep you?
Trina I don't think he would have asked me to marry him if he couldn't.
Jenny (*sitting* L *of the table*) Maybe he thinks you are going to keep *him*.
Mama (*warningly*) Jenny!
Sigrid Maybe he thinks Trina will have a dowry like the girls at home.
Trina Well, why shouldn't I? You all had dowries . . .
Jenny We were married in Norway. And our parents were alive. Where would your dowry come from, I'd like to know?
Trina Uncle Chris. He's head of the family.
Jenny And who will ask him?
Trina He won't need asking. When Mr Thorkelson goes to see him . . .
Jenny Uncle Chris will eat him!
Sigrid (*giggling maliciously*) Little Peter and Uncle Chris!
Mama (*with meaning*) Maybe Uncle Chris will tell him some family stories. He knows many, does Uncle Chris.

The Aunts put down their cups, discomfited

Jenny (*to change the subject*) Where are the children? Aren't we going to see them before we go?
Papa Of course. I'll call them. (*He goes to the door and does so, shouting*) Children! Your aunts are *leaving*!
Children's Voices (*eagerly shouting back*) Coming, Papa!
Jenny (*rising*) You come with us, Trina?

Sigrid rises

Mama I think maybe Trina like to stay here and listen to Mr Hyde read to us. You like, Trina?
Trina (*rising*) Well, if I wouldn't be in the way. I asked Mr Thorkelson to call for me here. He'll see me home. I'll help you with the coffee things.

She takes the tray of coffee cups and goes into the pantry. Katrin enters up L. *She carries her diary. Dagmar follows her, and behind them, Christine*

Katrin } (*together; curtsying*) Good evening, Aunt Sigrid. Good evening,
Dagmar }   Aunt Jenny.

Christine sketches a perfunctory curtsy without speaking

Jenny Where have *you* all been hiding yourselves?
Dagmar (*going into the pantry*) We've been in Christine's boodwar.
Jenny Her *what*?
Mama Christine makes the little closet into a boudoir. I give her those bead portières, Jenny, that you lend us when we come from the old country.
Sigrid And what does she do there?
Christine (*impertinently*) What people usually do in boudoirs.
Mama Christine, that is rude. It is her little place to herself.

Nels enters up L

Nels Hello, Aunt Sigrid. Hello, Aunt Jenny. (*He comes down* L)
Sigrid (*crossing to Nels, shaking hands*) Good evening, Nels. My, how tall
   he is getting!
Mama (*proudly*) Yes, is almost as tall as his Papa.

Nels sits on the chest under the window

Sigrid He looks to me as if he was outgrowing his strength. Dagmar was
   looking pale, too.

Dagmar enters up R. *She is carrying the cat*

(*Sigrid jumps*) Goodness, what a horrid-looking cat.
Dagmar She's not. She's beautiful.
Papa Is her new friend. She goes with Dagmar everywhere.
Christine (*sitting* L, *above the table*) She does. First thing you know, she'll
   have the cat sleeping with her.
Dagmar (*eagerly*) Oh, Mama, can I? Can I, Mama? (*She comes to the
   bench and sits*)
Jenny Certainly not. Don't you know a cat draws breath from a sleeping
   child? You wouldn't want to wake up some morning *smothered*, would
   you?
Dagmar I wouldn't care. Elizabeth can have *all* my breath! (*She blows
   into the cat's face*) There!
Jenny (*putting on her gloves*) Elizabeth—what a very silly name for a cat.
Nels (*rising*) It's a very silly name for *that* cat. It's a tom.
Mama Nels, how you know?
Nels I looked!
Dagmar How can you tell?
Nels You can.
Dagmar But how?
Mama (*quickly warning*) Nels, you do not say how!
Nels (*to Dagmar*) So you'd better think up another name for him.
Dagmar I won't. He's Elizabeth. And he's going to *stay* Elizabeth.
Papa We could call him *Uncle* Elizabeth!
Dagmar (*laughing delightedly*) Uncle Elizabeth! Do you hear, Elizabeth?
   You're called *Uncle* Elizabeth now!
Jenny Such foolishness! Well, good-bye, all. Marta. Lars.

Good-byes are exchanged all around, the Children curtsy formally

Mama (*crossing to the door* L) Good-bye, Jenny. Good-bye, Sigrid. Nels,
   you go tell Mr Hyde we are ready for the reading.

Nels goes off up L. *The Aunts go out* L *and walk down* L. *Mama stands
in the doorway, waving good-bye*

Sigrid (*as they go*) Well, I never thought we'd live to see Trina get married.

Jenny She's not married yet. She's got Uncle Chris to deal with first.

They disappear into the wings L. *Mama returns into the room and crosses to the door up* R

Mama (*calling into the pantry*) Trina, they have gone. Dagmar, you put Elizabeth out for the night now.
Dagmar (*correcting her*) *Uncle* Elizabeth!
Mama *Uncle* Elizabeth.

Dagmar goes out into the pantry with the cat. Trina comes in as Mr Hyde, carrying a book, and Nels enter up L

Mr Hyde, this is my sister Trina.
Mr Hyde (*bowing*) Enchanted!
Mama (*seating herself* R *of the table*) Mr Hyde reads to us *The Tales From Two Cities*. Is beautiful story. But sad.
Trina (*brightly*) I like sad stories. (*She gets out her handkerchief*)

The whole family group themselves around the table, Mama R *in her old chair, Papa fetches the chair from below the stove and sits above her, Trina* R *above the table, Nels* L *above the table. Dagmar enters and seats herself on the floor below Mama. Mr Hyde takes the armchair* L *of the table. Christine sits on the floor below the table. Katrin is on the steps down* R

Mr Hyde Tonight, I would like to finish it.
Mama Is good.
Mr Hyde Are you ready?
Children Yes, please, Mr Hyde.
Mr Hyde I will go on from where we left off. (*He starts to read*) "In the black prison of the Conciergerie, the doomed of the day awaited their fate. They were in number as the weeks of the year. Fifty-two were to roll that afternoon on the life-tide of the city to the boundless, everlasting sea . . ."

The Lights dim down slowly, leaving spots on Katrin and Mr Hyde only

Katrin I don't think I shall ever forget that night. It was almost midnight when he came to the end, and none of us had noticed.
Mr Hyde (*reading from the last page*) "It is a far, far better thing that I do than I have ever done; it is a far, far better rest that I go to than I have ever known." (*He closes the book*) "The End."

3 *The* R *turntable revolves in again. Katrin rises from and crosses to the step, her desk on the turntable*

Katrin I wrote in my diary that night before I went to bed. (*She reads aloud from it*) "Tonight Mr Hyde finished *The Tale of Two Cities*. The closing chapters are indeed superb. How beautiful a thing is self-sacrifice. I wish there were someone I could die for." (*She sits looking out front*) Mr Hyde read us all kinds of books. He thrilled us with *Treasure Island*, and terrified us with *The Hound of the Baskervilles*. I can still remember the horror in his voice as he read . . .

Mr Hyde (*still on the main stage in his spot: reading*) "Dr Mortimer looked strangely at us for an instant, and his voice sank almost to a whisper as he answered: 'Mr Holmes, they were the footprints of a gigantic *hound!*' " (*He closes the book*) We will continue tomorrow night. If you are interested.

Katrin (*looking out in front*) If we were interested! You couldn't have kept us from it. It meant a lot to Mama, too, because Nels stopped going nights to the street corner to hang about with the neighbourhood boys. The night they got into trouble for breaking into Mr Dillon's store, Nels was home with us. And sometimes Mr Hyde read us poetry. *The Lady of the Lake* and the *Rime of the Ancient Mariner*.

Mr Hyde (*reading*) "About, about, in reel and rout
The death-fires danced at night.
The water, like a witch's oils,
Burnt green and blue and white."

The Light on Mr Hyde goes out, and the TABS *close on the kitchen scene*

Katrin There were many nights I couldn't sleep for the way he had set my imagination dancing. (*Reading from her diary*) "What a wonderful thing is literature, transporting us to realms unknown." (*To herself*) And all the time my school teacher kept telling me that I ought to write about things I knew. I did write a piece for her once about Uncle Chris, and she said it wasn't nice to write like that about a member of one's own family. Papa called Mama's Uncle Chris a black Norwegian, because of his dark hair and fierce moustache, but there were others in the family who claimed that he was black in a different way. The aunts, for example.

The Light comes up on the L *turntable, representing Jenny's kitchen. Jenny* **4**
is rolling pastry. Trina is crocheting

Jenny Black! I'll say he's black. Black in his heart. Cursing and swearing . . .

Trina Marta says that's only because it hurts him to walk.

Jenny Rubbish. I know all about his limp and the accident back in the old country—but has anyone ever heard him complain? Marta's always making excuses for him.

Trina I know—but he *is* good to the children. All those oranges he's always sending them . . .

Jenny Oranges! What good is oranges? Turn 'em yellow. They're the only things he's ever been known to give away, anyway. He's got other uses for his money.

Trina What you mean?

Jenny Bottles! And that woman he lives with!

Trina He *says* she's his housekeeper.

Jenny Well, he couldn't very well come right out and call her what she is, could he? Though *I* will one of these days. And to his face, too.

Sigrid enters C *through the* TABS. *She crosses to Jenny and Trina*

Sigrid Jenny. Trina. What do you think? What do you think Uncle Chris has done now?

Trina What?

Jenny Tell us.

Sigrid You know my little Arne's knee—that fall he had two months ago? The man at the drugstore said it was only a bruise, but today it was hurting him again, so I left him home when I went to do the marketing. I asked Mrs Schultz next door to keep an eye on him, and who should turn up, not ten minutes after I'd gone, but Uncle Chris. And what do you think?

Jenny Well, tell us, if you're going to. Don't keep *asking* us.

Sigrid He took one look at Arne's knee, bundled him into that rattle-trap old automobile of his, and rushed him straight off to the hospital. I've just come from there. And what do you think? They've operated! They've got him in plaster of Paris!

Jenny Without consulting you?

Sigrid It seems the doctor is a friend of his . . . that's why he did it. No, this time he's gone too far. To put a child of Arne's age through all that pain. They wouldn't even let me *see* Arne. I'm going to tell Uncle Chris exactly what I think of him . . .

Jenny That's right.

Sigrid I'm going to tell him right now. (*Weakening a little*) Come with me, Jenny.

Jenny Well, I . . . No, I can't leave my baking.

Sigrid You must, Jenny. We must stand together. You come, too, Trina, and ask about your dowry. *Make* him give it to you.

Trina Oh, but—Marta said Mr Thorkelson should do that . . .

Jenny Well, then, go and get Mr Thorkelson. Go down to the mortuary and get him now. Sigrid is right. We girls have got to stand together!

Black-out. The turntable revolves out

Katrin (*at her desk*) Nobody knew where Uncle Chris lived. That was part of the mystery about him. He used to roam up and down the state buying up farms and ranches that had gone to pieces, and bullying them back into prosperity. Then he'd sell at a profit and move on again. Two or three times a year he'd descend on the city in his automobile and come roaring and stamping into our house.

The Light on Katrin dims

5   *The sound of a very old and noisy Ford car changing gears is heard off* L, *grinding and screaming as it comes to a standstill. Then Uncle Chris's voice, shouting*

Uncle Chris (*off*) Marta! Lars! Children—vere are you?

The TABS *part on the kitchen again. Outside in the street is Uncle Chris's car—an antique model. A woman is seated beside the empty driver's seat. Uncle Chris is knocking on the house door. He is an elderly, powerful, swarthy man with a limp. In the kitchen, Nels and Christine are cowering. A doctor's bag and hat are on the chest below the window*

Uncle Chris (*outside*) Marta! Lars!
Christine (*scared*) It's Uncle Chris.
Nels (*equally so*) I know.
Christine What'll we do?
Uncle Chris (*outside*) Is nobody home? Hey, there—is nobody home? (*Banging on the door*) Hey—someone—answer the door.

He tries the door handle, it opens and he strides, limpingly, in. He has a strong accent, and uses the Norwegian pronunciation of the children's names

So, vat is—you do not answer the door? You do not hear me calling?

The children cower silently

I say, you do not hear me calling? I do not call loud enough?
Christine Y-yes, Uncle Chris.
Uncle Chris Which yes? Yes, you do not hear me—or yes I do not call loud enough?
Nels We heard you, Uncle Chris.
Uncle Chris Then why you do not come?
Nels We—we were just going to.

Katrin has left her desk and come up the steps

Uncle Chris Let me look at you. You too, Katrinë, do not stand there—come and let me look at you. (*They line up down* C *as though for inspection. He thumps Nels between the shoulder-blades*) Stand tall! (*They all straighten up*) Um-hum. By the dresser, where the marks are.

Nels goes to the wall by the dresser up R. *Uncle Chris compares his mark with the previous one—and makes a new one on the wall, writing by it*

Two inches. Two inches in—(*examining the date*)—six months. Is good.

Nels comes down R. *Christine takes his place*

Christinë. Show me your teeth.

Christine opens her mouth

You brush them goot?

Christine nods

Nils, there is a box of oranges in the automobile. You fetch them in.

Nels crosses and goes out L

(*He measures Christine*) Where is the little von? Dagmar?
Katrin She's sick, Uncle Chris.
Uncle Chris (*arrested*) Sick? What is the matter with her?
Katrin It's her ear. She's had an earache for two days. Bad earache. Mama sent for the doctor.
Uncle Chris Goot doctor? What he say?

Katrin He's in there now. (*She points off, up* L)

Christine is standing by the wall, afraid to move

Uncle Chris I go in. (*He starts towards the door up* L)

Mama and Dr Johnson enter up L. *Christine and Katrin move down* R. *Nels has gone to the car, and with nervous smiles at the woman seated by the driver's seat, has heaved out a huge box of oranges. He returns with the oranges during the ensuing scene*

Mama (*to Uncle Chris*) Uncle Chris.

Uncle Chris How is with Dagmar?

Mama Is bad. Doctor, this is my uncle, Mr Halvorsen.

Doctor How do you do, sir? (*He goes to the chest below the window for his hat and bag*)

Uncle Chris What is with the child?

Doctor We must get her to a hospital. At once. We'll have to operate.

Mama Operate?

Doctor I'm afraid so.

Mama Can wait? Until my husband comes home from work?

Doctor I'm afraid not. Her best chance is for us to operate immediately.

Mama (*after a second*) We go. (*She goes to the dresser for the little bank*)

Uncle Chris (*who has watched her decision with approval, turns to the Doctor, moving to him down* L) What is with the child?

Doctor I'm afraid it's a mastoid.

Uncle Chris Ah—then you operate immediately.

Mama comes down to the table and empties the contents of the little bank on to it

Doctor (*resenting this*) That's what I said.

Uncle Chris Immediately!

Mama Doctor—is enough?

Doctor (*moving in to* L *of the table*) I was thinking of the County Hospital.

Mama No. No. We pay. Is enough?

Katrin If there isn't, we can go to the bank.

Christine We've got a bank account.

Mama Is enough without we go to the bank, Doctor? My husband is carpenter. Make good money.

Uncle Chris If there is need of money, *I* pay.

Doctor (*mainly in dislike of Uncle Chris*) It'll be all right. We'll take her to the Clinic. You pay what you can afford.

Uncle Chris Goot. Goot. I have a patient there already. My nephew, Arne. They operate this morning on his knee.

Doctor Are you a physician, sir?

Nels enters L *with the box of oranges*

Uncle Chris I am better physician than most doctors. Nils, there, my other nephew, he become doctor when he grow up.

Nels looks up, surprised. He puts the oranges on the table

Doctor (*chilly*) Oh, indeed—very interesting. Well, now, if you will have
the child at the Clinic in—shall we say an hour's time?

Uncle Chris (*striding across below the table*) The child will be at the Clinic
in *ten* minutes' time. I haf my automobile.

Doctor I can hardly make arrangements in ten minutes.

Uncle Chris (R *of the table*) *I* make arrangements. I know doctors.

Mama Uncle Chris. Dr Johnson arrange. He is good doctor.

Doctor (*ironically*) Thank you, madam.

Mama You go, Doctor. We come.

Doctor Very well, in an hour, then. And Dagmar will be well taken care
of, I promise you. I will do the operation myself.

Uncle Chris I watch.

Doctor You will do no such thing, sir.

Uncle Chris Always I watch operations. I am head of family.

Doctor I allow no-one to attend my operations.

Uncle Chris Are so bad?

Doctor (*to Mama*) Mrs Hanson, if I am to undertake this operation and the
care of your child, it must be on the strict understanding that this
gentleman does not come near either me or my patient.

Mama Yes, Doctor, I talk to him. You go to hospital now, please.

Doctor Very well. But you understand—nowhere near me, or I withdraw
from the case.

He goes out L, *down the street and into the wings*

Uncle Chris I go see Dagmar. (*He crosses above the table towards the door
up* L)

Mama (*stopping him above the table*) Wait. Uncle Chris, is kind of you, but
Dagmar is sick. You frighten her.

Uncle Chris I frighten her?

Mama Yes, Uncle Chris. You frighten everyone . . .

Uncle Chris (*amazed*) I?

Mama Everyone but me. Even the girls—Jenny, Sigrid, Trina—they are
frightened of you.

Uncle Chris The girls! Vomen! Pff!

Mama And the children, too. So Nels and I get Dagmar. You drive us
to hospital in your automobile, but you do not frighten Dagmar. And
you leave doctor alone. Dr Johnson is *fine* doctor. You come with me,
Nels. You carry Dagmar.

Nels and Mama go out up L. *Uncle Chris stands in amazement and puzzle-
ment. Katrin and Christine watch him, hardly daring to move*

Uncle Chris (*coming down* L *of the table*) Is true? I frighten you? Christinë
—Katrinë—you are frightened of me? Come, I ask you. Tell me the
truth. You are frightened of me?

Katrin (*tremulously*) A—little, Uncle Chris.

Uncle Chris (*sitting on the bench*) No? And you, Christinë?

Christine Y—yes, Uncle Chris.

Uncle Chris But Nils—Nils is a boy—he is not frightened?

Christine Not—not as much as we are . . .

Uncle Chris But he is frightened?

Christine Yes, Uncle Chris.

Uncle Chris (*with a roar*) But why? What is there to be frightened of? I am your Uncle Chris—why do I frighten you?

Christine I don't know.

Uncle Chris But that is bad. Very bad. The aunts, yes, I like to frighten them.

Katrin and Christine giggle

That makes you laugh. (*He rises and crosses to them*) You do not like the aunts? Come, tell me. You do not like the aunts? Say!

Katrin Not—very much, Uncle Chris.

Uncle Chris And which do you not like the most? Jenny—Sigrid—Trina. Tell me—huh?

Katrin I think I like Aunt Jenny least. She's so—so bossy.

Christine I can't stand Aunt Sigrid. Always whining and complaining.

Uncle Chris (*with a great roar of laughter*) Is good. Jenny, bossy. Sigrid, whining. Is true! But your mama, she is different. And she cook goot. The aunts, they cannot cook at all. Only you do not tell your mama we have talked of them so. It is a secret, for us. Then you cannot be frighted of me any more—when we have secret. I tell you my secret, too, *I* do not like the aunts. And so that they do not bother me, I frighten them and shout at them. You I do not shout at if you are goot children . . .

Jenny, Sigrid and Trina enter down L. *They are accompanied by Mr Thorkelson, a terrified little man. They move up to the street door*

And clean your teeth goot, and eat your oranges. (*He takes out a snuff-box and partakes of its cotents*)

Sigrid (*outside; stopping in the street*) Jenny. Do you see what I see? A woman, in his automobile.

Jenny (*outside*) How shameful!

Sigrid (*outside*) Ought we to bow?

Jenny (*outside*) Bow? To a woman like that? We cut her. That's what we do. I'll show you.

She strides to the front door, ignoring the woman in the car, and enters the house. Sigrid, Trina and Mr Thorkelson follow

Uncle Chris, Sigrid has something to say to you.

Sigrid (*with false bravery*) Uncle Chris, you took Arne to the hospital . . .

Uncle Chris (R *of the table*) Yes, I take Arne to the hospital. And now we take Dagmar to the hospital, so you do not clutter up the place.

Jenny (L *of the table*) What's the matter with Dagmar?

Christine It's her ear. Dr Johnson's going to operate.

Sigrid (*catching her favourite word*) Operate? This is some more of Uncle Chris's doing. Did you hear what he did to Arne?

Uncle Chris (*turning on her*) Sigrid, you are a whining old fool, and you get out of here . . .

Sigrid (*deflating*) We'd better go, Jenny . . .

Jenny (*stoutly*) No—there has been enough of these high-handed goings-on . . .

Uncle Chris And you, Jenny—you are a bossy old fool, and you get out of here, too, and we take Dagmar to hospital.

Nels enters up L, *carrying Dagmar in his arms, wrapped in a blanket*

You got her goot, Nils?

Nels Sure, Uncle Chris.

Uncle Chris (*crossing* L *to the street door*) We go.

Jenny (*getting between him and the door*) No! You are going to hear me out. (*Weakening*) That is, you are going to hear *Sigrid* out . . .

Uncle Chris If you do not get out of the way of the door before I count three, I trow you out. And Sigrid, too, as big as she is. Von . . .

Sigrid moves

Two . . .

Jenny moves

(*He looks back at the children with a wink and a smile*) Is goot! You put her in back of the car, Nils.

Nels goes out, L, *carrying Dagmar, and lifts her into the car. Uncle Chris follows. He cranks the car*

Trina runs to the door after him, with Mr Thorkelson

Trina But, Uncle Chris, I want to introduce Mr Thorkelson . . .

Uncle Chris ignores her, continuing to crank. Trina returns crestfallen into the room with Mr Thorkelson

Mama enters up L, *wearing her hat and coat and carrying a cheap little overnight case*

Mama Jenny—Trina, we go to hospital. (*She goes to Katrin and Christine*) You will be good children until Mama comes home?

Katrin
Christine } (*together*) Sure, Mama.

Uncle Chris (*outside; calling from the car*) Marta, we go!

Mama (*calling*) I come! (*She turns to the children again*) There is milk in the cooler, and fruit and cookies for your lunch.

Christine We'll be all right, Mama. Don't worry.

Mama I go now. (*She starts for the door*)

Sigrid (*stopping her*) Marta!
Mama What is it?
Sigrid You *can't* go in his automobile.
Mama Why not?
Uncle Chris (*outside, calling*) Marta, we go!
Mama I come!
Sigrid Because—because *she's* in it. The—the woman!
Mama So it will kill me, or Dagmar, if we sit in the automobile with her?
I have see her. She looks nice woman. (*Calling off, as she goes*) I come!

She goes out L into the street

Uncle Chris (*outside*) We go!

Mama climbs into the rear of the car, which backs noisily off during the next speeches

Mr Thorkelson (*in a low whisper to Trina*) Is that woman his wife?
Trina (*nervously*) Yes ...
Mr Thorkelson Yes?
Trina (*whispering back, loudly*) No!
Jenny (*to Katrin and Christine*) Don't stand there gaping like that, girls.
(*She shoos them into the pantry*) Go away! Go away!

Katrin and Christine go out up R

Jenny turns and sees the disappearing car through the open door
Oh! They've gone! We go after them! Sigrid, you lead the way.

Jenny gives Sigrid a push. Sigrid goes out L. Jenny follows, dragging Mr Thorkelson, and Trina comes last

Black-out. The TABS close

6   *The Light comes up on the R turntable, representing a kind of closet-room.*
Roller-skates are hanging on the wall. Katrin is seated on the floor and Christine on a small kitchen stepladder. They each have a glass of milk and a plate of biscuits

Katrin How long have they been gone now?
Christine About three hours. And I wish you wouldn't keep asking that.
Katrin How long do operations take? I heard Aunt Sigrid telling about Mrs Bergman who was five hours on the table.
Christine Aunt Sigrid's friends always have everything worse than anyone else. And it gets worse each time she tells it, too.

Katrin smiles, drinks some milk and eats a biscuit

Katrin (*with a certain melancholy enjoyment*) The house feels lonesome, doesn't it without Mama? It's like in a book. "The sisters sat huddled in the empty house, waiting for the verdict that was to spell life or death to the little family."

Christine Oh, don't talk such nonsense.

Katrin It's not nonsense.

Christine It is, too. In the first place, we're not a little family. We're a big one. And who said anything about life or death, anyway? Always trying to make everything so dramatic!

Katrin Well, it *is* dramatic.

Christine It's not. It's just . . . well, worrying. But you don't have to make a tragedy out of it.

There is a pause

Katrin You're not eating anything.

Christine I know that.

Katrin You're not drinking your milk, either. Aren't you hungry?

Christine No. And you wouldn't be, either, if you'd any feeling for Mama and Dagmar, instead of just heartlessly sitting there eating and enjoying making a story out of it.

Katrin Oh, Chris, I'm not heartless. I do have feeling for them. I can't help it if it goes into words like that. Everything always does with me. But it doesn't mean I don't feel it. And I think we *ought* to eat. I think Mama would want us to.

Pause. Christine hesitates a moment, then takes a bite of biscuit. They both eat in silence. The Light dims on them, and the turntable revolves out

The TABS *open on the hospital corridor. The back wall of the corridor runs   7 diagonally from up* R *to down* L. *At the downstage end is the lift-door.*

Immediately above this is a bench, on which Mama and Nels are sitting holding hands. Above the bench is a cupboard for brooms and mops. There is a reception desk, behind which a Nurse is sitting, at RC. *Down* R *Sigrid, Jenny and Trina are haranguing Uncle Chris. Mr Thorkelson stands slightly behind them*

Sigrid But, Uncle Chris, I tell you I must see him!

Uncle Chris (*storming*) You don't understand English? No visitors for twenty-four hours.

Sigrid But *you've* seen him.

Uncle Chris I am not visitor. I am exception.

Sigrid Well, then, his mother should be an exception, too. I'll see the doctor.

Uncle Chris *I* have seen doctor. I have told him you are not goot for Arne.

Sigrid Not good for my own son . . .

Uncle Chris Not goot at all. You cry over him. I go now.

He starts to go, but Jenny pushes Trina forward

Trina (*with desperate courage*) Uncle Chris . . . Uncle Chris . . . I *must* speak to you.

Uncle Chris I have business.

Trina But, Uncle Chris—I want to get married.

Uncle Chris Well, then *get* married. (*He starts off again*)

Trina No, wait, I—I want to marry Mr Thorkelson. Here. (*She produces* *him from behind her*) Peter, this is Uncle Chris. Uncle Chris, this is Mr Thorkelson.

Uncle Chris (*staring at Mr Thorkelson*) So?

Mr Thorkelson How are you, sir?

Uncle Chris Busy. (*He turns again*)

Trina Please, Uncle Chris . . .

Uncle Chris What is? You want to marry him? All right, marry him. I have other things to think about.

Trina (*eagerly*) Then—then you give your permission?

Uncle Chris Yes, I give my permission. If you want to be a fool, I cannot stop you.

Trina (*gratefully*) Oh, thank you, Uncle Chris.

Uncle Chris So. Is all?

Trina (*anxious to escape*) Yes, I think is all.

Jenny (*firmly*) No!

Uncle Chris No?

Mr Thorkelson is pushed forward again

Mr Thorkelson Well, there—there was a little something else. You see, Trina mentioned . . . well, in the old country, it was always usual . . . and after all, we do all come from the old country . . .

Uncle Chris What is it? What you want?

Mr Thorkelson Well, it's a question of Trina's . . . well, not to mince matters . . . her dowry.

Uncle Chris (*shouting*) Her what?

Mr Thorkelson (*very faintly*) Her dowry . . .

Uncle Chris Ah. Her dowry. Trina wants a dowry. She is forty-two years old——

Trina (*interrupting*) No, Uncle Chris . . .

Uncle Chris (*without pausing*) —and it is not enough she gets husband. She must have dowry.

Nurse (*who has been trying to interrupt, banging on her desk and moving down* R) *Please!* Would you mind going and discussing your family matters somewhere else? This is a hospital, not a marriage bureau.

Uncle Chris glares at the Nurse

Uncle Chris (*turning to Mr Thorkelson*) You come into waiting-room. I talk to you about dowry.

He strides off into the darkness behind the Nurse's desk. Mr Thorkelson, with an appealing look back at Trina, follows him

The Aunts now remember Mama, sitting on the bench, and cross to her

Jenny Did you hear that, Marta?

Mama (*out of a trance*) What?

Jenny Uncle Chris.

Mama No, I do not hear. I wait for doctor. Is two hours since they take Dagmar to operating-room. More.

Sigrid Two hours? That's nothing! When **Mrs Bergman** had her gall bladder removed she was *six* hours on the table.

Mama Sigrid, I do not want to hear about Mrs Bergman. I do not want to hear about anything. I wait for doctor. Please, you go away now. You come this evening.

Trina But, Marta, you can't stay here all by yourself.

Mama I have Nels. Please, Trina . . . I wait for doctor . . . you go now.

Jenny We go.

Trina Oh, but I must wait for Peter and Uncle Chris . . .

Jenny We'll go next door and have some coffee. Sigrid, do you have money?

Sigrid Yes, I—I have a little.

Jenny Good. Then I treat you. We'll be next door if you want us, Marta.

Mama nods without looking at them, her eyes still fixed on the lift door

The Aunts leave, going down the steps from the stage as though they were the hospital steps, and off L. *For a moment, the stage is quiet, then a Charwoman enters down* R. *She carries a mop and pail, puts it into the cupboard, and then goes. The lift door opens and a Doctor in a white coat comes out, followed by an Orderly, carrying a tray of dressings. They disappear up* R *behind the desk. Mama rises, agitatedly, looking after them. Then Dr Johnson enters down* R *carrying his hat and bag. He sees Mama and crosses to her*

Doctor Oh, Mrs Hanson . . .

Mama Doctor . . .

Doctor Well, Dagmar's fine. She came through it beautifully. She's back in bed now, sleeping off the anaesthetic.

Mama Thank you, Doctor. (*She shakes hands with him*)

Doctor You're very welcome.

Mama Is good of you, Doctor. (*She shakes hands with him again*) Where is she? I go to her now.

Doctor Oh, I'm sorry, but I'm afraid that's against the rules. You shall see her tomorrow.

Mama Tomorrow? But, Doctor, she is so little. When she wakes she will be frightened.

Doctor The nurse will take care of her. Excellent care. You needn't worry. You see, for the first twenty-four hours, clinic patients aren't allowed to see visitors. The wards must be kept quiet.

Mama I will not make a sound.

Doctor I'm very sorry. Tomorrow. And now—(*he glances at his watch*)—good afternoon.

He puts on his hat and goes down the steps and off L

Mama stands still a moment, looking after him

Mama Come, Nels. We go find Dagmar.

Nels But, Mama, the doctor said——

Mama We find Dagmar. (*She looks vaguely around her. Then goes to the Nurse's desk*) You tell me, please, where I can find my daughter?
Nurse What name?
Mama Dagmar.
Nels Dagmar Hanson.
Nurse (*looking at her record book*) Hanson, Ward A. Along there. (*She points upstage*)

Mama starts upstage

Oh, just a moment.

Mama returns

When did she come in?
Mama This morning. They just finish operation.
Nurse Oh, well, then, I'm afraid you can't see her today. No visitors for the first twenty-four hours.
Mama I'm not a visitor. I am her mama.
Nurse I'm sorry, but it's against the rules.
Mama Just for one minute. Please.
Nurse I'm sorry, but it's against the rules.

Mama stands staring. Nels touches her arm. She looks at him, nods, trying to smile, then turns and walks with him to L and down the steps

Mama We must think of some way.
Nels Mama, they'll let you see her tomorrow. They said so.
Mama If I don't see her today how will I know that all is well with her? What can I tell Papa when he comes home from work?
Nels The nurses will look after her, Mama. Would you like to come next door for some coffee?
Mama (*shaking her head*) We go home. We have coffee at home. But I must see Dagmar today.

She plods off L with Nels

The TABS *close*

8   *The Light comes up on the* R *turntable, representing a waiting-room. Uncle Chris is seated on a bench,* R, *and Mr Thorkelson is seated on a chair,* L. *There is a table with a potted plant between them. A clock on the wall tells the time as 2.30 p.m.*

Uncle Chris Well, it comes then to this. You love my niece, Trina?

Mr Thorkelson, very scared, gulps and nods

You want to marry her?

Mr Thorkelson nods again

You are in position to support her?

Mr Thorkelson nods again

Why, then, you want dowry?

Mr Thorkelson does not answer

(*Shouting*) What for you want dowry?
Mr Thorkelson Well—well, it would be a nice help. And it is customary.
Uncle Chris Is not customary. Who give dowries? Parents. Why? Because they are so glad they will not have to support their daughters any more, they pay money. I do not support Trina. I do not care if Trina gets married. Why then should I pay to have her married?
Mr Thorkelson I never thought of it like that.
Uncle Chris Is insult to girl to pay dowry. If I do not give dowry, will you still marry Trina?
Mr Thorkelson I—I don't know.
Uncle Chris You don't know? You don't know? You think I let Trina marry a man who will not take her without dowry?
Mr Thorkelson No, I suppose you wouldn't.
Uncle Chris What kind of man would that be? I ask you, what kind of man would that be?
Mr Thorkelson (*fascinated, helpless*) Well, not a very nice kind of man.
Uncle Chris And are you that kind of man?
Mr Thorkelson I—I don't think so.
Uncle Chris (*conclusively*) Then you don't want dowry!
Mr Thorkelson (*giving up*) No, I . . . I guess I don't.
Uncle Chris (*slapping his back*) Goot. Goot. You are goot man. I like you. I give you my blessing. And I send you vedding present. I send you box of oranges! (*He shakes Mr Thorkelson boisterously by the hand*)

Black-out. The turntable revolves out

The TABS *open on the kitchen. It is empty. Mama and Nels come up the hill* **9**
from the L *and let themselves into the house. There is silence as they take off their hats and coats*

Mama (*coming down* L; *after a moment*) Where are the girls?
Nels I guess they're upstairs. (*He goes to the door up* L *and calls*) Chris! Katrin!
Katrin ⎱ (*together*) Coming!
Christine ⎰
Nels Shall I make you some coffee? (*He crosses to the door up* R)

Mama shakes her head

You said you'd have coffee when you got home.
Mama (*sitting on the bench below the table*) Later. First I must think.
Nels (*coming down* R) Mama, please don't worry like that. Dagmar's all right. You know she's all right.

Katrin and Christine enter up L

Christine (*trying to be casual*, R *of the table*) Well, Mama, everything all right?
Mama (*nodding*) Is all right. You have eaten?
Katrin (L *of the table*) Yes, Mama.

Mama You drink your milk?
Christine Yes, Mama.
Mama Is good.
Christine (*seeing her face*) Mama, something's the matter.
Katrin (*over-dramatically*) Mama, Dagmar's not . . .? She isn't . . .?
  Mama!
Mama No, Dagmar is fine. The doctor say she is fine. (*She rises*) What is
  time?
Nels It's three o'clock.
Mama Three hours till Papa come home.

She looks around and then goes slowly out into the pantry, up R

Katrin (*crossing to Nels*) Nels, what is it? There *is* something the matter.
Nels They wouldn't let Mama see Dagmar. It's a rule of the hospital.
Christine But Dagmar's all right?
Nels Oh, yes, she's all right.
Christine (*impatiently*) Well, then . . .!
Nels But Mama's very upset. She started talking to me in Norwegian in
  the street-car.
Katrin (*emotionally*) What can we do?
Christine (*coldly*) You can't do anything. When *will* they let her see
  Dagmar?
Nels Tomorrow.
Christine Well, then, we'll just have to wait till tomorrow.
Katrin Chris, how can you be so callous? Can't you see that Mama's heart
  is breaking?
Christine No. I can't. And you can't, either. People's hearts don't break.
Katrin They do, too.
Christine Only in books.

Mama enters up R. *She wears an apron, and carries a scrubbing-brush and
a bucket of hot water*

Why, Mama, what are you going to do?
Mama (*coming down* R *of the table*) I scrub the floor. (*She gets down on her
  knees, facing front*)
Christine But you scrubbed it yesterday.
Mama I scrub it again. (*She starts to do so*)
Katrin But, Mama . . .
Mama (*bending low*) Comes a time when you've got to get down on your
  knees.
Katrin (*to Christine*) Now do you believe me?

*Christine, suddenly unendurably moved, turns and rushes from the room,
by the door up* L

Nels Mama, don't. Please don't. You must be tired.
Katrin (*strangely*) Let her alone, Nels.

They stand in silence watching her scrub. Suddenly Mama stops

What is it, Mama? What is it?

Mama (*sitting on her haunches*) I tink of something! (*Slowly*) I tink of something!

The Lights dim and the TABS *close on the kitchen*

Uncle Chris is heard singing from down L. *The Lights slowly come up on* **10**
the L *turntable, showing Arne, a child of about eight, in a hospital bed.*
Uncle Chris is seated on a chair beside the bed

Uncle Chris (*singing*) Ten t'ousand Svedes vent t'rough de veeds
                            At de battle of Coppen-hagen.
                            Ten t'ousand Svedes vent t'rough de veeds
                            Chasing vun Nor-ve-gan!

Arne Uncle Chris!

Uncle Chris Yes, Arne?

Arne Uncle Chris, does it *have* to hurt like this?

Uncle Chris If you vant it to be vell, and not to valk alvays like uncle Chris, it does—for a little. Is very bad?

Arne It is—kinda . . . Oo—oo . . .!

Uncle Chris Arne, don't you know any svear vords?

Arne W-what?

Uncle Chris Don't you know any svear vords?

Arne N-no, Uncle Chris. Not real ones.

Uncle Chris Then I tell you two fine vons to use when pain is bad. Are "Damn" and "Damittohell". You say them.

Arne N-now?

Uncle Chris No, not now. When pain comes again. You say them then. They help plenty. I know. I haf pain, too. I say them all the time. And if pain is *very* bad, you say, "*God*damittohell". But only if is *very* bad. Is bad now?

Arne No, it's—it's a little better.

Uncle Chris You sleep some now, maybe?

Arne I'll try. Will—will you stay here, Uncle Chris?

Uncle Chris Sure. Sure. I stay here. You are not frightened of Uncle Chris?

Arne No. Not any more.

Uncle Chris Goot. Goot. You like I sing some more?

Arne If you wouldn't mind. But maybe something a little . . . well, quieter.

Uncle Chris (*tenderly*) Sure. Sure.

He begins quietly to sing a Norwegian lullaby, in the midst, Arne cries out

Arne Oo—oo . . . Oh, *damn*. Damn. Damittohell!

Uncle Chris (*delighted*) Goot. It helps—eh?

Arne (*with pleased surprise*) Yes—yes.

Uncle Chris Then you sleep some!

He fixes Arne's pillows for him, and resumes the lullaby, seated on his chair beside the bed. After another verse, he leans over, assuring himself that the child is asleep, and then very quietly, without interrupting his singing, takes a flask from his pocket and lifts it to his lips

The Lights dim and the turntable revolves out

11 *The* TABS *open on the hospital corridor. There is a different Nurse now at the reception desk. She is talking on the telephone. Mama and Katrin enter down* L *and go up the steps*

Mama (*in an undertone*) Is not the same nurse. Katrin, you take my hat and coat. (*She takes them off, revealing that she still wears her apron*)
Katrin But, Mama, won't they——
Mama (*interrupting, finger to lips*) Ssh! You let me go ahead. You wait on bench for me.

She goes to the cupboard door above the bench and opens it. Katrin stares after her in trepidation. Mama takes out a damp mop and pail, and gets down on her knees by the Nurse's desk, starting to clean the floor. The Nurse looks up, and Mama catches her eye

(*Brightly*) Very dirty floors.
Nurse Yes, I'm glad they've finally decided to clean them. Aren't you working late?
Mama (*quickly, lowering her head*) Floors need cleaning.

She pushes her way, crawling on hands and knees, up behind the desk, and disappears up the corridor, still scrubbing

Katrin steals to the bench, and sits, still clutching Mama's hat and coat, looking interestedly around her. The Lights dim, leaving her in a single spot, as she starts to talk to herself

Katrin (*to herself*) "The Hospital" . . . A poem by Katrin Hanson. (*She starts to improvise*)
    She waited, fearful in the hall,
       And held her bated breath.
    Breath—yes, that'll rhyme with death. (*She repeats the first two lines*)
    She waited, fearful in the hall
       And held her bated breath.
    She trembled at the least footfall,
       And kept her mind on death.

She takes a piece of paper and a pencil from her pocket and begins to scribble

A Nurse comes out of the lift, carrying some charts, which she takes to the desk, and then goes out down R

Katrin goes on with her poem

    Ah, God, 'twas agony to wait.
       To wait and watch and wonder . . .
    Wonder—under—bunder—funder—sunder. Sunder! (*She nods to herself and goes on again*)

To wait and watch and wonder,
About her infant sister's fate.
If Death life's bonds would sunder.
(*Then to herself again, looking front*) That's beautiful. Yes, but it isn't true. Dagmar isn't dying. It's funny—I don't want her to die—and yet when Mama said she was all right I was almost—well, almost disappointed. It wasn't exciting any more. Maybe Christine's right, and I haven't any heart. How awful! "The girl without a heart." That'd be a nice title for a story. "The girl without a heart sat in the hospital corridor . . ."

The Lights come up again

Uncle Chris appears, up R *behind the desk. He wears his hat and is more than a little drunk. He sees Katrin*

Uncle Chris (*crossing towards Katrin*) Katrinë! What you do here? (*He sits on the bench beside her*)
Katrin (*nervously*) I'm waiting for Mama.
Uncle Chris. Where is she?
Katrin (*scared*) I—I don't know.
Uncle Chris What you mean—you don't know?
Katrin (*whispering*) I think—I think she's seeing Dagmar.
Uncle Chris (*shaking his head*) Is first day. They do not allow visitors first day.
Katrin (*trying to make him aware of the Nurse*) I know. But I think that's where she is.
Uncle Chris Where is Dagmar?
Katrin I don't know.

Uncle Chris rises and goes to the Nurse at the desk

Uncle Chris In what room is my great-niece, Dagmar Hanson?
Nurse (*looking at her book*) Hanson . . . Hanson . . . when did she come in?
Uncle Chris This morning.
Nurse Oh, yes. Were you wanting to see her?
Uncle Chris What room is she in?
Nurse I asked were you wanting to see her.
Uncle Chris And *I* ask what room she is in.
Nurse We don't allow visitors the first day.
Uncle Chris Have I said I vant to visit her? I ask what room she is in.
Nurse Are you by any chance, Mr . . . —(*looking at her book*)—Halvorsen?
Uncle Chris (*proudly, and correcting her pronunciation*) Christopher Halvorsen.
Nurse Did you say you were her uncle?
Uncle Chris Her great-uncle.
Nurse Well, then, I'm afraid I can't tell you anything about her.
Uncle Chris Why not?
Nurse Orders.

Uncle Chris Whose orders?

Nurse Dr Johnson's. There's a special note here. Patient's uncle, Mr Halvorsen, not to be admitted or given information under any circumstances.

Uncle Chris (*after a moment's angry stupefaction*) Goddamittohell! (*He strides away down* L, *taking out his flask, and shaking it, only to find it empty*)

Mama enters up R, *carrying the mop and pail, walking now and smiling triumphantly*

Mama (*to the Nurse*) Thank you. (*She replaces the mop and pail in the closet, and then sees Uncle Chris. She crosses to him*) Uncle Chris, Dagmar is fine!

Uncle Chris (*amazed*) You see her?

Mama Sure, Uncle Chris, I see her.

Uncle Chris (*reiterating; incredulous*) You see Dagmar?

Mama Sure. (*She takes her hat from Katrin and starts to put it on*) Is fine hospital. But such floors! A mop is never good. Floors should be scrubbed with a brush. We go home. Uncle Chris, you come with us? I make coffee.

Uncle Chris (*joining them in a little group on the steps down* L) Pah! Vot goot is coffee! I go get drink.

Mama (*reprovingly*) Uncle Chris!

Uncle Chris Marta, you are fine woman. Fine. But I go get drink. I get drunk.

Mama (*quickly aside to Katrin*) His leg hurts him.

Uncle Chris And you do not make excuses for me! I get drunk because I like it.

Mama (*conciliating him*) Sure, Uncle Chris.

Uncle Chris (*shouting*) I like it! (*Then, with a change*) No, is not true. You know is not true. I do not like to get drunk at all. But I do not like to come home with you, either. (*Growing slightly maudlin*) You have family. Is fine thing. You do not know how fine. Katrinë, one day when you grow up, maybe you know what a fine thing family is. I haf no family.

Katrin (*on the lower step*) But, Uncle Chris, Mama's always said you were the *head* of the family.

Uncle Chris Sure. Sure. I am head of the family, but I haf no family. So I go get drunk. You understand, Marta?

Mama Sure, Uncle Chris. You go get drunk. (*Sharply*) But don't you feel sorry for yourself!

Uncle Chris glares ar her a moment, then strides down the steps and off R, *boisterously singing his song of "Ten Thousand Swedes"*

Mama watches him go, then takes her coat from Katrin

Is fine man. Has fine ideas about family.

Katrin helps her on with her coat

I can tell Papa now that Dagmar is fine. She wake while I am with her.
I explain rules to her. She will not expect us now until tomorrow
afternoon.

Katrin You won't try and see her again before that?

Mama (*gravely*) No. That would be against the rules! Come. We go
home.

Katrin and Mama go off L

CURTAIN

ACT II

When the CURTAIN *rises, Katrin is at her desk on the* R *turntable*

Katrin (*reading*) "It wasn't very often that I could get Mama to talk—about herself, or her life in the old country, or what she felt about things. You had to catch her unawares, or when she had nothing to do, which was very, very seldom. I don't think I can ever remember seeing Mama unoccupied." (*She lays down the manuscript and looks out front*) I do remember one occasion, though. It was the day before Dagmar came home from the hospital. And as we left, Mama suggested treating me to an ice-cream soda. (*She rises, gets her hat from beside her—a school-girl hat—puts it on and crosses to* C *while she speaks the next lines*) She had never done such a thing before, and I remember how proud it made me feel—just to sit and talk to her quietly like a grown-up person. It was a kind of special treat-moment in my life that I'll always remember—quite apart from the soda, which was *wonderful*. (*She is now* C)

Mama enters C *through the* TABS *and comes down the steps*

Mama Katrin, you like we go next door, and I treat you to an ice-cream soda?
Katrin (*young now, and overcome*) Mama—do you mean it?
Mama Sure. We celebrate. We celebrate that Dagmar is well, and coming home again.

13 *They cross* L, *where the turntable represents a drugstore, with a table and two chairs at which they seat themselves. Mama is* L *of the table*

What you like to have, Katrin?
Katrin (*with desperate earnestness*) I think a chocolate . . . no, a strawberry . . . no, a chocolate soda.
Mama (*smiling*) You are sure?
Katrin (*gravely*) I think so. But, Mama, can we *afford* it?
Mama I think this once we can afford it.

The Soda Clerk appears from the L

Soda Clerk What's it going to be, ladies?
Mama A chocolate ice-cream soda, please—and a cup of coffee.

The Soda Clerk goes

Katrin Mama, he called us "ladies"!

Mama smiles

Why aren't you having a soda, too?

Mama Better I like coffee.

Katrin When can I drink coffee?

Mama When you are grown up.

Katrin When I'm eighteen?

Mama Maybe before that.

Katrin When I graduate?

Mama Maybe. I don't know. Comes the day you are grown up. Papa and I will know.

Katrin Is coffee really nicer than a soda?

Mama When you are grown up, it is.

Katrin Did you used to like sodas better—before you were grown up?

Mama We didn't have sodas before I was grown up. It was in the old country.

Katrin (*incredulously*) You mean they don't have sodas in Norway?

Mama Now, maybe. Now I think they have many things from America. But not when I was little girl.

The Soda Clerk brings the soda and the coffee

Soda Clerk There you are, folks.

He sets them down and departs

Katrin (*after a good pull at the soda*) Mama, do you ever want to go back to the old country?

Mama I like to go back once to look, maybe. To see the mountains and the fjords. I like to show them once to you all. When Dagmar is big, may be we all go back once—one summer—like tourists. But that is how it would be. I would be tourist there now. There is no-one I would know any more. And maybe we see the little house where Papa and I live when we first marry. And—(*her eyes grow misty and reminiscent*)— something else I would look at.

Katrin What is that?

Mama does not answer

What would you look at, Mama?

Mama Katrin, you do not know you have brother? Besides Nels?

Katrin No! A brother? In Norway? Mama . . .

Mama He is my first baby. I am eighteen when he is born.

Katrin Is he there now?

Mama (*simply*) He is dead.

Katrin (*disappointed*) Oh. I thought you meant . . . I thought you meant a real brother. A long-lost one, like in stories. When did he die?

Mama When he is two years old. It is his grave I would like to see again. (*She is suddenly near tears, biting her lip and stirring her coffee violently, spilling some. She gets her handkerchief from her handbag, dabs at her skirt, then briefly at her nose, then she returns the handkerchief and turns to Katrin again. Matter-of-factly*) Is good, your ice-cream soda?

Katrin (*more interested now in Mama than in it*) Yes. Mama—have you had a very *hard* life?

Mama (*surprised*) Hard? No. No life is easy all the time. It is not meant to be. (*She pours the spilled coffee back from the saucer into her cup*)

Katrin But—rich people—aren't *their* lives easy?

Mama I don't know, Katrin. I have never known rich people. But I see them sometimes in stores and in the streets, and they do not *look* as if they were easy.

Katrin Wouldn't you like to be rich?

Mama I would like to be rich the way I would like to be ten feet high. Would be good for some things—bad for others.

Katrin But didn't you come to America to *get* rich?

Mama (*shocked*) No. We come to America because they are all here—all the others. Is good for families to be together.

Katrin And did you like it right away?

Mama Right away. When we get off the ferry boat and I see San Francisco and all the family, I say: "Is like Norway", only it is better than Norway. And then you are all born here, and I become American citizen. But not to get rich.

Katrin *I* want to be rich. Rich and famous. I'd buy you your warm coat. When are you going to get that coat, Mama?

Mama Soon now, maybe—when we pay doctor, and Mr Hyde pay his rent. I think now I *must* ask him. I ask him tomorrow, after Dagmar comes home.

Katrin When I'm rich and famous, I'll buy you lovely clothes. White satin gowns with long trains to them. And jewellery, I'll buy you a pearl necklace.

Mama We talk too much! (*She sighs to the Soda Clerk offstage*) Come, finish your soda. We must go home.

The Soda Clerk appears

How much it is, please?

Soda Clerk Fifteen cents.

Mama Here are two dimes. You keep the nickel. And thank you. Was good coffee. (*They start up the steps towards the* TABS c) Tomorrow Dagmar will be home again. And, Katrin, you see Uncle Elizabeth is there. This afternoon again she was asking for him. You keep Uncle Elizabeth in the house all day until she comes home.

They disappear through the TABS

14 *After a second, the howls of a cat in pain are heard from behind the* CURTAINS —*low at first, then rising to a heart-rending volume, and then diminishing again as the* TABS *part on the kitchen once more. Mama, Papa and Dagmar are entering the house*

Dagmar (*standing on the threshold, transfixed*) It's Uncle Elizabeth, welcoming me home! That's his song of welcome. Where is he, Mama? (*She looks around for the source of the howls*)

Mama (*taking off her coat and putting it on the chest*) He is in the pantry.

Dagmar starts to rush off up R

But wait—wait a minute, Dagmar. I must tell you. Uncle Elizabeth is—sick.

Dagmar Sick? What's the matter with him?

Papa He has been in fight. Last night. He come home this morning very sick indeed. (*He comes down* L, *takes off his coat and hat and puts them on the chest*)

Dagmar crosses to the pantry door, as Nels enters by it

Mama Nels, how is Uncle Elizabeth? Nels has been doctoring him.

Nels He's pretty bad, Mama. I've dressed all his wounds again with boric acid, but . . .

Dagmar tries to get past him

I wouldn't go and see him now, baby.

Dagmar I've got to. He's my cat. I haven't seen him in a whole month. More.

She runs out into the pantry

Mama (*coming above the table*) Nels, what you think?

Nels I think we ought to have had him put away before she came home.

Mama But she would have been so unhappy if he was not here *at all*.

Nels She'll be unhappier still if he dies.

Another howl is heard from the pantry, and then Dagmar comes rushing back

Dagmar (*running to Mama*) Mama, what happened to him? What happened to him? Oh, Mama—when I tried to pick him up, his bandage slipped over his eye. It was bleeding. Oh, Mama, it looked awful. Oh . . . (*She starts to cry*)

Mama (*fondling her*) He looks like that all over. Nels, you go to see to his eye again.

Wearily, Nels returns to the pantry

Listen, Dagmar . . . *Lille Ven* . . . would it not be better for the poor thing to go quietly to sleep?

Dagmar You mean—go to sleep and never wake up again?

Mama nods gently

No.

Papa I think he die, anyway. Nels try to make him well. But I do not think he can.

Dagmar Mama can. Mama can do everything.

There is another howl from off-stage. Dagmar clutches Mama agonizedly

Make him live, Mama. Make him well again. *Please!*
Mama We see. Let us see how he gets through the night. And now, Dagmar, you must go to bed. I bring you your supper.
Dagmar But you will fix Uncle Elizabeth? You promise, Mama?
Mama I promise I try. Go now.

Dagmar goes out up L

I must fix her supper.

She moves towards the pantry up R. *There are more howls. Papa and Mama stand and look at one another*

Nels enters up R

Nels Mama, it's just cruelty, keeping that cat alive.
Mama I know.

There is another howl, the longest yet

Papa You say we see how the cat get through the night. I ask you how do *we* get through the night? Is no use, Marta. We must put the cat to sleep. Nels, you go to the drugstore, and get something. Some chloroform, maybe. (*He holds out a coin*)
Nels How much shall I get? (*He crosses to Papa and takes the coin*)
Papa You ask the man. You tell him it is for a cat. He knows.

Nels goes out L *and down the street into the wings, with a look at Mama's face*

Is best. Is the only thing.
Mama I know. But poor Dagmar. It is sad homecoming for her. And she has been so good in hospital. Never once she cry. (*She pulls herself together*) I get her supper.

There is another howl

And I take the cat outside. Right outside, where we . . . where *Dagmar* cannot hear him.

She goes out up R *into the pantry*

Papa takes a folded newspaper from his pocket, puts on his glasses and sits in the chair L *of the table. He starts to read*

The door up L *opens gently and Mr Hyde peeps in. He wears his hat and coat and carries his suitcase and a letter. Papa has his back to him. Mr Hyde lays the letter on the dresser and then starts to tiptoe to the street door* L. *Then Papa sees him*

Papa You go out, Mr Hyde?

Mr Hyde (*pretending surprise*) Oh . . . Oh, I did not see you, Mr Hanson. (*He puts down the suitcase*) I did not know you were back. As a matter of fact, I—I was about to leave this letter for you. (*He fetches it*) The fact is—I—I have been called away.

Papa So?

Mr Hyde A letter I received this morning necessitates my departure. My immediate departure.

Papa I am sorry.

Mama enters up R *with a tray, on which are milk, bread, butter and jelly*

Mama, Mr Hyde says he goes away.

Mama (*coming to the table with the tray*) Is true?

Mr Hyde Alas, dear madam, yes. 'Tis true, 'tis pity. And pity 'tis, 'tis true. You will find here—(*he presents the letter*)—my cheque for all I owe you, and a note expressing my profoundest thanks for all your most kind hospitality. You will say good-bye to the children for me?

He bows

Mama (*taking the letter; distressed*) Sure. Sure.

Mr Hyde (*bowing again*) Madam, my deepest gratitude.

He kisses her hand. Mama looks astonished. He bows to Papa

Sir, my sincerest admiration! (*He opens the street door*) It has been a privilege. *Ave Atque Vale!* Hail and Farewell!

He makes a gesture and goes off

Mama Was wonderful man! Is too bad. (*She opens the letter and takes out the cheque*)

Papa How much is cheque for?

Mama Hundred ten dollar! Is four months.

Papa Good. Good.

Mama Is wonderful. Now we pay doctor everything.

Papa And you buy your warm coat. With fur now, maybe.

Mama (*sadly*) But there will be no more reading. You take the cheque, Lars. You get the money?

Papa (*taking it*) Sure. I get it. What does he say in his letter?

Mama You read it while I fix supper for Dagmar. (*She starts to butter the bread, and spread jelly*)

Papa (*reading*) "Dear Friends—I find myself compelled to take a some-what hasty departure from this house of happiness . . ."

Mama Is beautiful letter.

Papa "I am leaving you my library for the children . . ."

Mama He leaves his books?

Papa He says so.

Mama But is wonderful. Go see, Lars. See if they are in his room.

Papa lays down the letter, rises and goes out up L. *Nels and Christine appear down* L, *coming up the street. Christine carries some school books*

Christine (*outside*) I'm sure it was him, Nels. Carrying his suitcase, and getting on the cable-car. I'm sure he's going away.
Nels (*outside*) Well, I hope he's paid Mama.

They open the street door L *and enter the kitchen*

Christine (*bursting in*) Mama, I saw Mr Hyde getting on the cable-car.
Mama I know. He leave.
Christine Did he pay you?
Mama Sure, he pay me. Hundred ten dollar . . .
Nels Gee . . .
Mama (*smiling*) Is good.
Christine Are you going to put it in the bank?
Mama We need it right away.

Papa enters up L. *He staggers under an armful of books*

Mr Hyde leaves his books, too. For you.
Nels Say!

Papa stacks them on the table. Nels and Christine rush to them and read the titles

The Pickwick Papers, The Complete Shakespeare . . .
Christine *Alice in Wonderland, The Oxford Book of Verse . . .*
Nels *The Last of the Mohicans, Ivanhoe . . .*
Christine We were right in the middle of that.
Mama Nels can finish it. He can read to us now in the evenings. He has fine voice, too, like Mr Hyde.

Nels flushes with pleasure

Is wonderful. So much we can learn. (*She finishes the supper-making*) Christine, you take the butter back to the cooler for me, and the jelly, too.

Christine takes the butter and jelly and goes out up R

I go up to Dagmar now. (*She lifts the tray, then pauses*) You get it, Nels?
Nels What? Oh . . . (*He takes a druggist's small bottle from his pocket*) Here.
Mama You put it down. After I come back, we do it. You know how?
Nels Why, no, Mama, I . . . (*He puts the bottle on the table*)
Mama You do not ask?
Nels No. I—I thought Papa . . .
Mama You know, Lars?
Papa No, I don't know. But it cannot be difficult. If you *hold* the cat . . .

Jenny enters down L. *She comes up the street in a state of some excitement*

Mama And watch him die? No! I think better you get rags and a big sponge, to soak up the chloroform. You put it in the box with him, and cover him over. You get them ready out there
Nels Sure, Mama.
Mama I bring some blankets.

Nels goes out up R. *Christine enters up* R.

Mama lifts the tray and starts for the door up L. *Jenny knocks on the street door*

Mama (*agitated*) So much goes on! See who it is, Christine.
Christine (*crossing to the window and peeping*) It's Aunt Jenny. (*She opens the door*)

Jenny enters the kitchen

Mama Jenny . . .
Jenny (*breathless*) Marta—has he gone?
Mama (*above the table*) Who?
Jenny (*coming* L *of the table*) Your boarder—Mr Hyde . . .
Mama Yes, he has gone. Why?
Jenny Did he pay you?
Mama Sure he pay me.
Jenny How?
Mama He give me a cheque. Lars has it right there.
Jenny (*with meaning*) A cheque!
Mama Jenny, what is it? Christine, you give Dagmar her supper. I come soon.

Christine takes the tray from Mama and goes out up L

What is it, Jenny? How do you know that Mr Hyde has gone?
Jenny I was at Mr Kruper's down the street—you know, the restaurant and bakery—and he told me Mr Hyde was there today having his lunch, and when he left he asked if he would cash a cheque for him. For fifty dollars. (*She pauses*)
Papa Well, go on.
Jenny Your fine Mr Hyde didn't expect Mr Kruper to take it to the bank until tomorrow, but he did. And what do you think? Mr Hyde hasn't even an *account* at that bank!

Nels enters up R *and stands in the doorway*

Mama I don't understand.
Papa (*taking the cheque from his pocket*) You mean the cheque is no good?

Jenny No good at all. (*Triumphantly*) Your Mr Hyde was a crook, just as I always thought he was, for all his reading and fine ways. Mr Kruper said he'd been cashing them all over the neighbourhood.

Mama stands quite still, without answering

How much did he owe you? Plenty, I'll bet.

Mama still does not answer

Eh? Marta, I said I bet he owed you plenty. Didn't he?

Mama (*looking around, first at Nels and then down at the books on the table*) No. No, he owed us nothing. (*She takes the cheque from Papa and tears it across*) Nothing.

Jenny (*persistently*) How much was that cheque for? (*She reaches her hand for it*)

Mama (*evading her*) It does not matter. He pay with better things than money. (*She goes to the stove, throws the cheque into the flames and watches it burn*)

Jenny I told you right in the beginning that you shouldn't trust him. But you were so sure—just like you always are. Mr Hyde was a gentleman. A gentleman! I bet it must have been a hundred dollars that he rooked you of. Wasn't it?

Mama (*returning to the table*) Jenny, I cannot talk now. Maybe you don't have things to do. I have.

Jenny (*sneeringly*) What? What have *you* got to do that's so important?

Mama (*taking up the medicine bottle, fiercely*) I have to chloroform a cat!

Jenny steps back in momentary alarm, almost as though Mama were referring to her

Mama goes out up L with the medicine bottle, not so very unlike Lady Macbeth with the daggers

Black-out. The TABS *close*

15 *After a moment, the* TABS *open again on the kitchen. It is the next morning. The books have been taken off the table, and Mama is setting the breakfast dishes, with Papa helping her. Dagmar comes bursting into the room up L*

Dagmar Good morning, Mama. 'Morning, Papa. Is Uncle Elizabeth all better?

Mama Dagmar, there is something I must tell you.

Dagmar I want to see Uncle Elizabeth first.

She runs out

Mama turns helplessly to Papa

Mama Do something! Tell her!

Papa If we just let her think the cat die . . . by itself . . .

Mama No. We cannot tell her lies.

Papa goes to the door up R *and opens it*

Dagmar (*off*) What a funny, funny smell. Good morning, my darling, my darling Elizabeth.

Mama and Papa stand stricken

> *Dagmar enters, carrying the cat, wrapped in an old shirt, with its head covered. She comes down* R *of the table*

My goodness, you put enough blankets on him! Did you think he'd catch cold?

Mama (*horror-stricken*) Dagmar, you must not . . . (*She stops at the sight of the cat, whose tail is twitching, quite obviously alive*) Dagmar, let me see—let me see the cat! (*She crosses to her, below the table, and uncovers the cat's head*)

Dagmar (*overjoyed*) He's well. Oh, Mama, I *knew* you'd fix him.

Mama (*appalled*) But, Dagmar, I didn't. I . . .

Dagmar (*ignoring her*) I'm going to take him right up and show him to Nels.

She runs off up L

(*Off*) Nels! Nels! Uncle Elizabeth's well again.

Mama (*turning to Papa*) Is a miracle! (*She sits, dumbfounded, on the bench below the table*)

Papa (*coming down beside her, shrugging*) You cannot have used enough chloroform. You just give him good sleep, and that cures him. We rechristen the cat, Lazarus!

Mama But, Lars, we must tell her. Is not *good* to let her grow up believing I can fix *everything*!

Papa Is best thing in the world for her to believe. (*He chuckles*) Besides, I know *exactly* how she feels. (*He lays his hand on hers*)

Mama (*rising and turning with embarrassment from his demonstrativeness and slapping his hand*) We finish getting breakfast. (*She turns back to the table*)

The TABS *close*

The Lights on the stage down R *come up. Katrin and Christine enter down* R. **16**
They wear school clothes and hats. Christine carries some school books in a strap. Katrin is reciting

Katrin The quality of mercy is not strained,
>   It droppeth as the gentle rain from heaven
>   Upon the place beneath: it is twice blest;
>   It blesseth him that gives, and him that takes . . .

(*She dries up*) . . . him that takes. It blesseth him that gives and him that takes . . . (*She turns to Christine*) What comes after that?

Christine I don't know. And I don't care.

Katrin Why, Chris!

Christine I don't. It's all I've heard for weeks. The school play, and your graduation, and going on to High. And never a thought of what's happening at home.

Katrin What do you mean?

Christine You see—you don't even know!

Katrin Oh, you mean the strike?

Christine Yes, I mean the strike. Papa hasn't worked for four whole weeks, and a lot you care. Why, I don't believe you even know what they're striking *for*. Do you? All you and your friends can talk about is the presents you're going to get. You make me ashamed of being a girl.

Two girls, Madeline and Dorothy, enter c, *through the* TABS, *talking*

Madeline (*to Dorothy*) Thyra Walsh's family's going to add seven pearls to the necklace they started for her when she was a baby. Oh, hello, Katrin! Did you hear about Thyra's graduation present?

Katrin (*not very happily*) Yes, I heard.

Madeline I'm getting an onyx ring, with a diamond in it.

Katrin A real diamond?

Madeline Yes, of course. A *small* diamond.

Dorothy What are *you* getting?

Katrin Well—well, they haven't actually told me, but I think—I think I'm going to get that pink celluloid dresser set in your father's drug-store.

Dorothy You mean that one in the window?

Katrin (*to Madeline*) It's got a brush and comb and mirror—and a hair-receiver. It's genuine celluloid!

Dorothy I wanted Father to give it to me, out of stock, but he said it was too expensive. Father's an awful tightwad. They're giving me a bangle.

Madeline Oh, there's the street-car. We've got to fly. 'Bye, Katrin. 'Bye, Christine. See you tomorrow. Come on, Dorothy.

Dorothy and Madeline rush off L

Christine Who said you were going to get the dresser set?

Katrin Nobody's said so—for certain. But I've sort of hinted, and . . .

Christine (*going up the steps*) Well, you're not going to get it.

Katrin How do you know?

Christine (*turning*) Because I know what you *are* getting. I heard Mama tell Aunt Jenny. Aunt Jenny said you were too young to appreciate it.

Katrin What is it?

Christine Mama's giving you her brooch. Her *solje*.

Katrin You mean that old silver thing she wears that belonged to Grand-mother? What would I want àn old thing like that for?

Christine It's an heirloom. Mama thinks a lot of it.

Katrin Well, then, she ought to keep it. You don't really mean that's *all* they're going to give me?

Christine What more do you want?

Katrin I want the dresser set. My goodness, if Mama doesn't realize what's a suitable present . . . why, it's practically the most important time in a girl's life, when she graduates.
Christine And you say you're not selfish!
Katrin It's not selfishness.
Christine Well, I don't know what else you'd call it. With Papa not working, we need every penny we can lay our hands on. Even the little bank's empty. But you'll devil Mama into giving you the dresser set somehow. So why talk about it? I'm going home.

She turns and goes through the TABS

Katrin stands alone with a set and stubborn mouth, and then sits on the steps

Katrin Christine was right. I got the dresser set. They gave it to me just before supper on graduation night. Papa could not attend the exercises because there was a strike meeting to decide about going back to work. I was so excited that night I could hardly eat, and the present took the last remnants of my appetite clean away.

The TABS *open on the kitchen. Papa, Mama and Dagmar are seated at the* 17
table, with coffee. Christine is clearing dishes

Christine I'll just stack the dishes now, Mama. We'll wash them when we come home.

She goes out with them up R

Papa (R *of the table. Holding up a cube of sugar*) Who wants coffee-sugar?
(*He dips it in his coffee*) Dagmar? (*He hands it to her*) Katrin?
Katrin rises from the steps and moves up into the scene for the sugar
Mama (L *of the table*) You get your coat, Katrin; you need it.

Katrin goes out up L

Dagmar (*above the table*) Aunt Jenny says if we drank black coffee like you do at our age, it would turn our complexions dark. I'd like to be a black Norwegian. Like Uncle Chris. Can I, Papa?
Papa I like you better blonde. Like Mama.
Dagmar When do you get old enough for your complexion *not* to turn dark? When can we drink coffee?
Papa One day, when you are grown up.

Jenny and Trina have entered down L *and move up to the street door* L.
Jenny knocks

Mama There are Jenny and Trina. (*She rises and goes to the door*) Is good. We can start now. (*She opens the door*)

Jenny and Trina enter

Papa She always meant it for you, Katrin. And you must not cry. You have your play to act.

Katrin (*sobbing*) I don't want to act in it now.

Papa But you must. Your audience is waiting.

Katrin (*as before*) I don't care.

Papa But you must care. Tonight you are not Katrin any longer. You are an actress. And an actress must act, whatever she is feeling. There is a saying—what is it . . .

Trina (*brightly*) The mails must go through!

Papa No, no. The show must go on. So stop your crying, and go and act your play. We talk of this later. Afterwards.

Katrin (*pulling herself together*) All right, I'll go.

Sniffing a good deal, she picks up the dresser set and goes out into the street and off down L

Papa and Trina exchange glances. Papa sits R of the table and they settle down to their checkers

Papa Now we play.

The Lights fade. The TABS close

18 *Lights come up on the R turntable, representing a makeshift dressing-room. Dorothy and Madeline are dressing in costumes for "The Merchant of Venice"*

Dorothy I'm getting worried about Katrin. If anything's happened to her . . .

Madeline (*pulling up her tights*) I'll forget my lines. I know I will. I'll look out and see Miss Forrester sitting there, and forget every single line.

Katrin rushes in from the L. She carries the dresser set and places it on the dressing-table

We thought you'd had an accident, or something . . .

Katrin Dorothy, is your father here tonight?

Dorothy He's going to be. Why?

Katrin I want to speak to him. (*As she pulls off her hat and coat*) Will you tell him—please—not to go away without speaking to me? After. After the exercises.

Dorothy What on earth do you want to speak to Father for?

Katrin I've got something to say to him. Something to ask him. It's important. Very important.

Madeline Is that the dresser set? (*Picking it up*) Can I look at it a minute?

Katrin (*snatching it from her, violently*) No!

Madeline Why, what's the matter? I only wanted to look at it.

Katrin (*emotionally*) You can't. You're not to touch it. Dorothy, you take it and put it where I can't see it. (*She thrusts it at her*) Go on . . . Take it! Take it! Take it!

Black-out

The Tabs *open on the kitchen. Mama and Papa are in conclave at the table* **19**
with cups of coffee

Mama (*seated above the table*) I am worried about her, Lars. When it is
over, I see her talking with Mr Schiller—and then she goes to take off
her costume and Nels tells me that he will bring her home. But it is long
time, and is late for her to be out. And in the play, Lars, she was not
good. I have heard her practice it here, and she was good, but tonight,
no. It was as if—as if she was thinking of something else all the time.

Papa (*seated* R *of the table*) I think maybe she was.

Mama But what? What can be worrying her?

Papa Marta—tonight, after you leave, Katrin found out about your
brooch.

Mama My brooch? But how? Who told her?

Papa Christine.

Mama (*angrily*) Why?

Papa I do not know.

Mama (*rising with a sternness we have not seen before, and calling*) Christine! Christine! (*She moves* L *of the table*)

Christine enters up R. *She is wiping a dish*

Christine Were you calling me, Mama? (*She comes a little down* R)

Mama Yes. Christine, did you tell Katrin tonight about my brooch?

Christine (*frightened, but firmly*) Yes.

Mama Why did you?

Christine Because I hated the smug way she was acting over that dresser
set.

Mama Is no excuse. You make her unhappy. You make her not good in
the play.

Christine Well, she made you unhappy, giving up your brooch for her
selfishness.

Mama (*crossing towards Christine, above the table*) Is not your business. I
choose to give my brooch. Is not for you to judge. And you know I do
not want you to tell. I am angry with you, Christine.

Christine I'm sorry. But I'm not sorry I told.

She goes back to the pantry up R *with a set, obstinate face*

Papa Christine is the stubborn one.

Nels and Katrin have appeared down L *and moved up to the house. They*
stop and look at each other in the lamplight. Katrin looks scared. Then
Nels pats her, and she enters, Nels follows

Mama looks up inquiringly and searchingly into Katrin's face. Katrin turns
away, taking off her hat and coat, and taking something from her pocket.
She puts her hat and coat on the chest

Nels (*crossing above the table*) What happened at the meeting, Papa?
Papa We go back to work tomorrow.
Nels Gee, that's bully. Isn't it, Mama?
Mama (*sitting L of the table; absently*) Yes, is good.
Katrin (*coming to Mama*) Mama—here's your brooch. (*She gives it to her*) I'm sorry I was so bad in the play. I'll go and help Christine with the dishes.

She turns and goes out up R

Mama (*unwrapping the brooch from tissue paper*) Mr Schiller give it back to her?
Nels We went to his house to get it. He didn't want to. He was planning to give it to his wife for her birthday. But Katrin begged and begged him. She even offered to go and work in his store during her vacation if he'd give it back.
Papa (*impressed*) So? So?
Mama And what did Mr Schiller say?
Nels He said that wasn't necessary. But he gave her a job all the same. She's going to work for him, afternoons, for three dollars a week.
Mama And the dresser set—she gave that back?
Nels Yes. She was awful upset, Mama. It was kinda hard for her to do. She's a good kid. Well, I'll say good night. I've got to be up early.
Papa Good night, Nels.
Nels Good night, Papa.

He goes out up L

Mama Good night, Nels.
Papa Nels is the kind one. (*He starts to re-fill Mama's coffee cup*)

Mama stops him, putting her hand over her cup

No?
Mama (*rising, crossing up R and calling*) Katrin! Katrin!

Katrin appears in the door up R

Katrin Yes, Mama?
Mama (*sitting R above the table*) Come here.

Katrin comes to her

(*She holds out the brooch*) You put this on.
Katrin No—it's yours.
Mama It is your graduation present. I put it on for you. (*She pins the brooch on Katrin's dress*)
Katrin (*near to tears*) I'll wear it always. I'll keep it for ever.
Mama Christine should not have told you.
Katrin (*moving away down R*) I'm glad she did. Now.

Papa And I'm glad, too. (*He dips a lump of sugar and holds it out to her*) Katrin?

Katrin (*tearful again, shaking her head*) I'm sorry, Papa. I—I don't feel like it. (*She crosses below the table and sits on the chest under the window, with her back to the room*)

Papa So? So? (*He rises and goes to the dresser*)

Mama What you want, Lars?

Papa does not answer. He takes a cup and saucer, comes to the table and pours a cup of coffee, indicating Katrin with his head. Mama nods, pleased, then checks his pouring and fills up the cup from the cream jug which she empties in so doing. Papa puts sugar in, and crosses to Katrin

Papa Katrin. (*He holds out the cup*)

Katrin turns

Katrin (*incredulously*) For me?

Papa For our grown-up daughter.

Mama nods, standing arm in arm with Papa. Katrin takes the cup, lifts it— then her emotion overcomes her

Katrin thrusts the cup at Papa and rushes from the room

(*As he crosses to the table and puts down the cup*) Katrin is the dramatic one! Is too bad. Her first cup of coffee, and she does not drink it.

Mama It would not have been good for her, so late at night.

Papa (*smiling*) And you, Marta, you are the practical one.

Mama You drink the coffee, Lars. We do not want to waste it. (*She pushes it across to him*)

The Lights dim. The TABS *close*

The Lights come up on the L *turntable, representing the parlour of Jenny's* **20** *house. There is a table with a telephone on it. Trina is speaking into the phone*

Trina Yes, Peter. . . . Yes, Peter. . . . I know, Peter, but we don't know where he is. It's so long since we heard from him. He's sure to turn up soon. Yes, I know, Peter. I know, but . . . (*Subsiding obediently*) Yes, Peter. . . . Yes, Peter.

Jenny enters behind her, eating a piece of toast and jam

(*Sentimentally*) Oh, Peter, you know I do. Good-bye, Peter. (*She hangs up, turns and sees Jenny*)

Jenny What was all that about?

Trina Peter says we shouldn't wait any longer to hear from Uncle Chris. He says we should send the wedding invitations out right away. He was quite insistent about it. Peter can be very masterful sometimes . . . when he's alone with me!

The telephone rings. Jenny answers it. She puts down the toast. Trina picks it up and nibbles at it during the scene

Jenny This is Mrs Stenborg's boarding-house. Mrs Stenborg speaking. . . . Oh, yes, Marta—what is it? . . . (*She listens*)

21 *The Lights come up on the* R *turntable, disclosing Mama standing at a wall telephone booth. She wears a hat and coat, and has an opened telegram in her hand*

Mama Jenny, is Uncle Chris. I have a telegram. It says if we want to see him again we should come without delay.

Jenny Where is he?

Mama (*consulting the telegram*) It comes from a place called Ukiah. Nels says it is up north from San Francisco.

Jenny Who is the telegram from?

Mama It does not say.

Jenny That—woman?

Mama I don't know, Jenny. I think maybe.

Jenny I won't go.

Sigrid enters C *through the* TABS. *She wears a hat and coat and carries a string bag full of vegetables*

(*Whispering to Sigrid*) It's Uncle Chris. Marta says he's dying. (*Into the phone*) Why was the telegram sent to you? I'm the eldest.

Mama Jenny, is not the time to think of who is eldest. Uncle Chris is dying.

Jenny *I* don't believe it. He's too mean to die. Ever.

Nels enters down R *and moves to Mama. He hands her a slip of paper*

I'm not going.

Mama Jenny, I cannot stop to argue. There is a train at eleven o'clock. It takes four hours. You call Sigrid.

Jenny Sigrid is here now.

Mama Good. Then you tell her.

Jenny What do you say the name of the place is?

Mama Ukiah. (*Spelling in Norwegian*) U-K-I-A-H.

Jenny I won't go.

Mama That *you* decide. (*She hangs up*)

The Lights on the R *turntable go out*

Sigrid Uncle Chris dying!

Jenny The wages of sin.

Trina Oh, he's old. Maybe it is time for him to go.

Jenny Four hours by train, and maybe have to stay all night. All that expense to watch a wicked old man die of the D.T.s.

Sigrid I know, but . . . there is his will . . .

Jenny Huh, even supposing he's anything to leave—you know who he'd leave it *to*, don't you?

Sigrid Yes. But all the same he's dying now, and blood is thicker than water. Especially when it's Norwegian. I'm going. I shall take Arne with me. Uncle Chris was always fond of children.

Trina I agree with Sigrid, I think we *should* go.

Jenny Well, *you* can't go, anyway.

Trina Why not?

Jenny Because of that woman. You can't meet a woman like that.

Trina Why not? If you two can . . .

Sigrid We're married women.

Trina I'm engaged!

Jenny That's not the same thing.

Sigrid Not the same thing at all!

Trina Nonsense. I've never met a woman like that. Maybe I'll never get another chance. Besides, if he's going to change his will, there's still my dowry, remember. Do you think we should take Peter?

Jenny Peter Thorkelson. Whatever for?

Trina Well, after all, I mean—I mean, his profession . . .

Jenny Trina, you always were a fool. Anyone would know the last person a dying man wants to see is an undertaker!

Black-out. The turntable revolves out

A Spot comes up on Katrin, standing down RC. *She wears her school-girl hat*   22

Katrin When Mama said I was to go with her, I was excited and I was frightened. It was exciting to take sandwiches for the train, almost as though we were going on a picnic. But I was scared at the idea of seeing death, though I told myself that if I was going to be a writer, I had to experience everything. But all the same, I hoped it would be all over when we got there. (*She walks towards* c *and up the steps*) It was afternoon when we arrived. We asked at the station for the Halvorsen ranch, and it seemed to me that the man looked at us strangely. Uncle Chris was obviously considered an odd character. The ranch was about three miles from the town; a derelict, rambling old place. There was long grass, and tall trees, and a smell of honeysuckle. We made quite a cavalcade, walking up from the gate.

The procession enters R, *behind Katrin: Mama, Jenny, Trina, Sigrid and Arne*

The woman came out on the steps to meet us.

The procession starts towards the c, *moving upstage*

The Woman comes through the TABS, *down one step*

The Aunts freeze in their tracks. Mama goes forward to her

Mama How is he? Is he . . . ?

Woman (*with grave self-possession*) Come in, won't you?

She holds the TABS *slightly aside. Mama goes in. Katrin follows, looking curiously at the Woman. The Aunts walk stiffly past her, Sigrid clutching Arne and shielding him from contact with the Woman. They disappear behind the TABS. The Woman stands a moment, looking off into the distance. Then she goes in through the TABS, too*

23   *The TABS open, revealing Uncle Chris's bedroom. It is simple, and shabby. The door to the room is L in the back wall. In the L wall is a window, with curtains, drawn aside now. In front of it, a wash-stand. The afternoon sunlight comes through the window, falling on the big double bed, in which Uncle Chris is propped up on pillows. Beside him, R, on a small table is a carafe of water. L of the bed there is a chair. He has a glass in his hand. Mama stands to the R of him, Jenny to the L. The others are ranged below the window. The Woman is not present*

Uncle Chris (*handing Mama the empty glass*) I want more. You give me more. Is still some in the bottle.
Mama Uncle Chris, that will not help now.
Uncle Chris It always help. (*With a glance at Jenny*) Now especially.
Jenny (*firmly*) Uncle Chris, I don't think you realize . . .
Uncle Chris What I don't realize? That I am dying? Why else do I think you come here? Why else do I think you stand there, watching me? (*He sits upright*) Get out. Get out. I don't want you here. Get out!
Jenny Oh, very well. Very well. We'll be outside on the porch, if you want us. (*She starts towards the door*)
Uncle Chris That is where I want you . . . on the porch!

Jenny goes out. Trina follows. Sigrid is about to go, too, when Uncle Chris stops her

Wait. That is Arne. Come here, Arne.

Arne, propelled by Sigrid, advances towards the bed

How is your knee?
Arne It's fine, Uncle Chris.
Uncle Chris Not hurt any more? You don't use svear vords any more?
Arne N-no, Uncle Chris.
Uncle Chris You walk goot? Quite goot? Let me see you walk. Walk around the room.

Arne does so

Fast. Fast. Run! Run!

Arne does so

Is goot.
Sigrid (*encouraged and advancing*) Uncle Chris, Arne has always been so fond of you . . .
Uncle Chris (*shouting*) I tell you all to get out. Except Marta.

Katrin edges with Sigrid to the door

And Katrinë. Katrinë and I haf secret. You remember, Katrinë?

Katrin Yes, Uncle Chris.

Mama Uncle Chris, you must lie down again.

Uncle Chris Then you give me drink.

Mama No, Uncle Chris.

Uncle Chris We cannot waste what is left in the bottle. You do not drink it . . . who will drink it when I am gone? What harm can it do—now? I die, anyway . . . You give it to me.

Mama crosses to the wash-stand, pours him a drink of whisky and water, and takes it to him, sitting on the bed beside him to the L of him. Katrin moves down L

(*He drinks, then turns to her, leaning back against her arm and the pillows*) Marta, I haf never made a will. Was never enough money. But you sell this ranch. It will not bring moch. I have not had it long enough. And there is mortgage. Big mortgage. But it leave a little. Maybe two, tree hundred dollars. You give to Yessie.

Mama Yessie?

Uncle Chris Yessie Brown. My housekeeper. No, why I call her that to you? You understand. She is my voman. Twelve years she has been my voman. My wife, only I cannot marry her. She has husband alive somewhere. She was trained nurse, but she get sick and I bring her to the country to get well again. There will be no money for *you*, Marta. Always I wanted there should be money to make Nils doctor. But there were other things—quick things. And now there is no time to make more. There is no money, but you make Nils doctor, all the same. You like?

Mama Sure, Uncle Chris. It is what Lars and I have always wanted for him. To help people who suffer . . .

Uncle Chris Is the greatest thing in the world. It is to have a little of God in you. Always I wanted to be doctor myself. Is the only thing I have ever wanted. Nils must do it for me.

Mama He will, Uncle Chris.

Uncle Chris Is goot. (*He strokes her hand*) You are the goot one. I am glad you come, *Lille Ven*. (*He moves his head restlessly*) Where is Yessie?

Mama I think she wait outside.

Uncle Chris You do not mind if she is here?

Mama Of course not, Uncle Chris.

Uncle Chris You call her I like you both be here.

Mama goes out, with a quick glance at Katrin

Katrin has been standing, forgotten, down L, listening intently. Uncle Chris signs to Katrin to come closer. She sits on the chair L of the bed

Katrinë, your mama write me you drink coffee now?

Katrin nods

(*He looks at her affectionately*) Katrinë, who will be writer . . . You are not frightened of me now?

Katrin No, Uncle Chris.

Uncle Chris One day maybe you write story about Uncle Chris. If you remember.

Katrin (*whispering*) I'll remember.

Mama enters with the Woman. Katrin rises. They come to the bed and stand on either side of it—Mama to the L

Uncle Chris (*obviously exhausted and in pain*) I like you both stay with me—now. I think now maybe Katrinë go away. Good-bye, Katrinë. (*He repeats it in Norwegian*) Farvell, Katrinë.

Katrin Good-bye, Uncle Chris.

Uncle Chris You say it in Norwegian, like I do.

Katrin *Farvell, Onkel* Chris.

She slips out of the room, in tears

Uncle Chris Yessie! Maybe I should introduce you to each other. Yessie, this is my niece, Marta. The only von of my nieces I can stand. Marta, this is Yessie, who have give me much happiness . . .

Mama and Jessie shake hands across the bed

Mama I am very glad to meet you.

Jessie I am, too.

Uncle Chris (*as they shake hands*) Is goot. And now you give me von more drink. You have drink with me—both of you. That way we finish the bottle. Yes?

Jessie and Mama look at each other

Mama Sure, Uncle Chris.

Uncle Chris Goot. Yessie, you get best glasses. (*With a chuckle to Mama*) Yessie does not like to drink, but this is special occasion.

Jessie gets three glasses from a wall shelf at R *and crosses with them to the wash-stand*

What is the time?

Mama It is about half-past four, Uncle Chris.

Uncle Chris The sun come around this side the house in afternoon. You draw the curtain a little maybe. Is strong for my eyes.

Mama crosses and draws the curtain over the window. The stage darkens. Jessie pours three drinks, filling two of the glasses with water. She is about to put water in the third when Uncle Chris stops her

No, no, I take it now without water. Always the last drink without water. Is Norwegian custom. (*To Mama, with a smile*) True?

Jessie crosses to the R *of the bed and sits on it beside Uncle Chris, about to feed his drink to him, but he pushes her aside*

No. No, I do not need you feed it to me. I can drink myself. (*He takes the glass from her*) Give Marta her glass.

Jessie hands a glass to Mama. The two women stand one each side of the bed, holding their glasses

So . . . Skoal!

Jessie (*clinking glasses with him*) Skoal.
Mama (*doing likewise*) Skoal.

They all three drink. The Lights dim slowly to a Black-out. The Tabs *close*

The Lights come up on the r *turntable showing a porch with a bench, and a* **24** *chair, on which the three Aunts are sitting. Jenny is dozing in the chair*

Sigrid (*flicking her handkerchief*) These gnats are awful. I'm being simply eaten alive.
Trina Gnats are always worse around sunset. (*She catches one*)
Jenny (*rousing herself*) I should never have let you talk me into coming. To be insulted like that—turned out of his room—and then expected to sit here hour after hour without as much as a cup of coffee . . .
Sigrid I'd make coffee if I knew where the kitchen was.
Jenny *Her* kitchen? It would poison me. (*Rising*) No, I'm going home. Are you coming, Trina?
Trina Oh, I think we ought to wait a little longer. After all, you can't *hurry* these things . . . I mean . . . (*She breaks off in confusion at what she has said*)
Jenny (*to Sigrid*) And all your talk about his will. A lot of chance we got to say a word!
Trina Maybe Marta's been talking to him.

Mama enters c *through the* Tabs

Jenny Well?
Mama Uncle Chris has—gone.

There is silence

Jenny (*more gently than is her wont*) Did he—say anything about a will?
Mama There is no will.
Jenny Well, then, that means—we're his nearest relatives . . .
Mama There is no money, either.
Sigrid How do you know?
Mama He told me. (*She brings out a small notebook that she is carrying*)
Jenny What's that?
Mama Is an account of how he spent the money.
Jenny Bills from a liquor store.
Mama No, Jenny. No. I read it to you.

Jenny sits

You know how Uncle Chris was lame—how he walked always with limp. It was his one thought—lame people. He would have liked to be doctor and help them. Instead, he help them other ways. I read you the last page . . . (*She reads from the notebook*) "Joseph Spinelli. Four years old. Tubercular left leg. Three hundred thirty-seven dollars, eighteen

cents." (*She pauses*) "Walks now. Esta Jensen. Nine years. Club-foot. Two hundred seventeen dollars, fifty cents. Walks now." (*Then, reading very slowly*) "*Arne* Solfeldt . . ."
Sigrid (*startled*) *My* Arne?
Mama (*reading on*) "Nine years. Fractured kneecap. Four hundred forty-two dollars, sixteen cents."

Katrin and Arne run in from the L across the stage

Arne (*calling*) Mother—Mother—are we going to eat soon? (*He stops, awed by the solemnity of the group*) What is it? Is Uncle Chris . . . ?

Mama puts out a hand gently to silence him

Mama (*to the Aunts*) It does not tell the end about Arne. I like to write "Walks now". Yes?
Sigrid (*very subdued*) Yes.
Mama (*taking a pencil from the book*) Maybe even—"runs"?

Sigrid nods, moist-eyed. Trina is crying. Mama writes in the book, then closes it

So. Is finished. Is all. (*She touches Jenny on the shoulder*) It was good.
Jenny (*after a gulping movement*) I go and make some coffee.

The Woman, Jessie, enters C through the TABS, and stands on the steps

Jessie You can go in and see him now if you want.

Jenny looks back, half-hesitant, at the others. Then she nods and goes in. Trina follows her, mopping her eyes. Sigrid puts her arm suddenly around Arne in a spasm of maternal affection, and they, too, go in

Mama and Jessie are left alone. Katrin stands LC

I'm moving down to the hotel for tonight—so that you can all stay. (*She is about to go through the TABS*)
Mama (*stopping her*) Wait. What will you do now—after he is buried? You have money?

Jessie shakes her head

Where you live?
Jessie I'll find a room somewhere. I'll probably go back to nursing.
Mama You like to come to San Francisco for a little? To our house? We have room. Plenty room.
Jessie (*touched, moving to Mama*) That's very kind of you, but . . .
Mama I like to have you. You come for a little as our guest. When you get work you can be our boarder.
Jessie (*awkwardly grateful*) I don't know why you should bother . . .
Mama (*touching her*) You were good to Uncle Chris.

Jessie grasps Mama's hand, deeply moved, then turns and goes quickly through the TABS

(*She turns to Katrin*) Katrin, you come and see him?
Katrin (*scared*) See him? You mean . . .
Mama I like you see him. You need not be frightened. He looks—happy and at peace. I like you to know what death looks like. Then you are not frightened of it, ever.
Katrin Will you come with me?
Mama Sure.

She stretches out her hand, puts her arm around Katrin, and leads her gently through the TABS

The Lights come up on the L *turntable, representing a park bench against a*   **25**
*hedge. Trina and Mr Thorkelson, in outdoor clothes, are seated together.
Trina is cooing over a baby-carriage*

Trina Who's the most beautiful Norwegian baby in San Francisco? Who's going to be three months old tomorrow? Little Christopher Thorkelson! (*To Mr Thorkelson*) Do you know, Peter, I think he's even beginning to *look* a little like Uncle Chris! Quite apart from his black curls—and those, of course, he gets from *you*. (*To the baby*) He's going to grow up to be a black Norwegian, isn't he, just like his Daddy and his Uncle Chris? (*Settling down beside Mr Thorkelson*) I think there's something about his mouth—a sort of—well—*firmness*. Of course, it's *your* mouth, too. But then I've always thought you had quite a lot of Uncle Chris about you. (*She looks back at the baby*) Look—he's asleep!
Mr Thorkelson Trina, do you know what next Thursday is?
Trina (*nodding, smilingly*) Our anniversary.
Mr Thorkelson What would you think of our giving a little party?
Trina A party?
Mr Thorkelson Oh, quite a modest one. Nothing showy or ostentatious—but, after all, we have been married a year, and with your having been in mourning and the baby coming so soon and everything, we've not been able to entertain. I think it's time you took your place in society.
Trina (*scared*) What—sort of a party?
Mr Thorkelson An evening party. (*Proudly*) A soirée! I should say about ten people—some of the Norwegian colony—and Lars and Marta, of course . . .
Trina (*beginning to count on her fingers*) And Jenny and Sigrid . . .
Mr Thorkelson Oh—I—I hadn't thought of asking Jenny and Sigrid.
Trina Oh, we'd have to. We couldn't leave them out.
Mr Thorkelson Trina, I hope you won't be offended if I say that I have never really felt—well, altogether comfortable with Jenny and Sigrid. They have always made me feel that they didn't think I was—well—*worthy* of you. Of course, I know I'm not, but—well—one doesn't like to be reminded of it—*all* the time.
Trina (*taking his hand*) Oh, Peter.
Mr Thorkelson But you're quite right. We must ask them. Now, as to the matter of refreshments—what would you suggest?
Trina (*flustered*) Oh, I don't know. I . . . what would you say to—ice-

cream and cookies for the ladies—and coffee, of course—and—perhaps
port wine for the gentlemen?

Mr Thorkelson (*anxiously*) Port wine?

Trina Just a little. You could bring it in already poured out, in *little*
glasses. Jenny and Sigrid can help me serve the ice-cream.

Mr Thorkelson (*firmly*) No. If Jenny and Sigrid come, they come as guests,
like everyone else. You shall have someone in to help you in the
kitchen.

Trina You mean a waitress?

Mr Thorkelson nods, beaming

Oh, but none of us have *ever* . . . do you really think . . . I mean . . .
you did say we shouldn't be ostentatious . . .

Mr Thorkelson (*nervously, rising and starting to pace up and down*) Trina,
there's something I would like to say. I've never been very good at
expressing myself or my—well—*deeper* feelings—but I want you to know
that I'm not only very fond of you, but very—well—very *proud* of you
as well, and I want you to have the best of everything, as far as it's in
my power to give it to you. (*He sits again—then, as a climax*) I want you
to have a waitress!

Trina (*overcome*) Yes, Peter.

26   *They hold hands. The Lights fade and the turntable revolves out*

*The TABS part on the kitchen, slightly changed, smartened and refurnished
now. Mama and Papa are seated as usual L and R of the table. Mama is
darning. Dagmar, looking a little older, is seated on the chest, reading a
solid-looking book. Nels enters up L, carrying a newspaper and a letter. He
wears long trousers now, and looks about seventeen*

Nels (*crossing and hitting Papa playfully on the head with the paper*) Hello!
Here's your evening paper, Papa.

*Papa puts down the morning paper he is reading, and takes the evening one
from Nels*

Papa Is there any news?

Nels No. (*He takes out a packet of cigarettes with elaborate unconcern*)
Mama watches with disapproval

(*He is about to light his cigarette, but stops, remembering something*) Oh,
I forgot. There's a letter for Katrin. I picked it up on the mat as I came
in. (*He goes to the door up L and calls*) Katrin! Katrin! There's a letter
for you.

Katrin (*off*) Coming!

Mama Nels, you know who the letter is from?

Nels (*coming down to Mama*) Why, no, Mama. (*He hands it to her*) It looks
like her own handwriting.

Mama (*gravely inspecting it*) Is bad.

Papa Why is bad?

Mama She get too many like that. I think they are stories she send to the
magazines.

Dagmar (*closing her book loudly and rising*) Well, I'll go and see if I have any puppies yet. (*She crosses below the table and then turns*) Mama, I've just decided something.

Mama What have you decided?

Dagmar If Nels is going to be a doctor, when I grow up, I'm going to be a—(*looking at the book-title, and stumbling over the word*)—vet-vet-veterinarian.

Mama And what is that?

Dagmar A doctor for animals.

Mama Is good. Is good.

Dagmar There are far more animals in the world than there are human beings, and far more human doctors than animal ones. It isn't fair. (*She crosses to the door up* R) I suppose we couldn't have a horse, could we?

This only produces a concerted laugh from the family

(*She turns, sadly*) No—I was afraid we couldn't.

She goes out up R. *Katrin enters up* L. *She wears a slightly more adult dress than before. Her hair is up and she looks about eighteen*

Katrin Where's the letter?

Mama (*handing it to her*) Here.

Katrin takes it, nervously. She looks at the envelope, and her face falls. She opens it, pulls out a manuscript and a rejection slip, looks at it a moment, and then replaces both in the envelope. The others watch her covertly. Then she looks up, with determination

Katrin (*above the table*) Mama—Papa—I want to say something.

Papa What is it?

Katrin I'm not going to go to college.

Papa Why not?

Katrin Because it would be a waste of time and money. The only point in my going to college was to be a writer. Well, I'm not going to be one, so . . .

Mama Katrin, is it your letter that makes you say this? It is a story come back again?

Katrin Again is right. This is the tenth time. I made this one a test. It's the best I've ever written, or ever shall write. I know that. Well, it's no good.

Nels (R *of Katrin*) What kind of a story is it?

Katrin Oh—it's a story about a painter, who's a genius, and he goes blind.

Nels Sounds like *The Light That Failed.*

Katrin Well, what's wrong with that?

Nels (*quickly*) Nothing. Nothing!

Katrin (*moving down* L) Besides, it's not like that. My painter gets better. He has an operation and recovers his sight, and paints better than ever before.

Mama Is good.

Katrin (*bitterly unhappy*) No, it isn't. It's rotten. But it's the best I can do.

Mama You have asked your teachers about this?

Katrin Teachers don't know anything about writing. They just know about literature. (*She crosses* R)

Mama If there was someone we could ask—for advice . . . to tell us—tell us if your stories are good.

Katrin Yes. Well, there isn't. And they're *not*

Papa (*looking at the evening paper*) There is something here in the paper about a lady writer. I just noticed the headline. Wait. (*He looks back for it and reads*) "Woman writer tells key to literary success."

Katrin Who?

Papa A lady called Florence Dana Moorhead. It gives her picture. A fat lady. You have heard of her?

Katrin Yes, of course. Everyone has. She's terribly successful. She's here on a lecture tour.

Mama What does she say is the secret?

Papa You read it, Katrin. (*He hands Katrin the paper*)

Katrin (*reading, gabbling the first part*) "Florence Dana Moorhead, celebrated novelist and short-story writer . . . blah-blah-blah . . . interviewed today in her suite at the Fairmont . . . blah-blah-blah . . . pronounced sincerity the one essential quality for success as a writer." (*She throws aside the paper*) A lot of help that is.

Mama Katrin, this lady . . . maybe if you sent her your stories, *she* could tell you what is wrong with them?

Katrin (*wearily*) Oh, Mama, don't be silly.

Mama Why is silly?

Katrin (*moving above the table*) Well, in the first place because she's a very important person—a celebrity—and she'd never read them. And in the second, because . . . you seem to think writing's like—well, like cooking, or something. That all you have to have is the recipe. It takes a lot more than that. You have to have a gift for it.

Mama You have to have a gift for cooking, too. But there are things you can learn, if you have the gift.

Katrin Well, that's the whole point. I haven't. I *know* now. So, if you've finished with the morning paper, Papa, I'll take the want-ad section, and see if I can find myself a job.

She takes the morning newspaper and goes out up L

Mama Is bad. Nels, what you think?

Nels I don't know, Mama. Her stories seem all right to me, but I don't know.

Mama It would be good to know. Nels, this lady in the paper . . . what else does she say?

Nels (*taking up the paper*) Not much. The rest seems to be about *her* and her home. Let's see . . . (*He reads, walking down* L) "Apart from literature, Mrs Moorhead's main interest in life is gastronomy."

Mama The stars?

Nels No—eating. "A brilliant cook herself, she says that she would as soon turn out a good soufflé as a short story, or find a new recipe as she would a first edition."

Mama (*reaching for the paper*) I see her picture? (*She looks at it*) Is kind face. (*Pause while she reads a moment. Then she looks up and asks*) What is first edition?

Black-out. The TABS *close*

The Lights come up on the L *turntable, representing the lobby of the Fair-*   **27**
mont Hotel. There is a couch against a column with a palm behind it. An orchestra plays softly in the background. Mama is discovered seated on the couch, waiting patiently. She wears a hat and a suit, and clutches a newspaper and a bundle of manuscripts. A couple of guests enter C *through the* TABS *and cross, disappearing into the wings* L. *Mama watches them. Then Florence Dana Moorhead enters through the* TABS. *She is a stout, dressy, good-natured, middle-aged woman. A Bell-boy enters from the* R, *paging her*

Bell-boy Miss Moorhead?
Miss Moorhead Yes? (*She stands, waiting on the steps*)
Bell-boy Telegram.
Miss Moorhead Oh. Thank you. (*She tips him*)

The Bell-boy exits R

Mama rises and moves towards Miss Moorhead

Mama Please—please—Miss Moorhead . . . Miss Moorhead.
Miss Moorhead (*looking up from her telegram*) Were you calling me?
Mama Yes. You are—Miss Florence Dana Moorhead?
Miss Moorhead Yes.
Mama Please—might I speak to you for a moment?
Miss Moorhead Yes—what's it about?
Mama I read in the paper what you say about writing.
Miss Moorhead (*with a vague social smile*) Oh, yes?
Mama My daughter, Katrin, wants to be writer.
Miss Moorhead (*who has heard that one before*) Oh, really? (*She glances at her watch on her bosom*)
Mama I bring her stories.
Miss Moorhead Look, I'm afraid I'm in rather a hurry. I'm leaving San Francisco this evening . . .
Mama I wait two hours here for you to come in. Please, if I may talk to you for one, two minutes. That is all.
Miss Moorhead (*kindly*) Of course, but I think I'd better tell you that if you want me to read your daughter's stories, it's no use. I'm very sorry, but I've had to make it a rule never to read anyone's unpublished material.

Mama nods

Mama (*after a pause*) It said in the paper you like to collect recipes . . . for eating.
Miss Moorhead Yes, I do. I've written several books on cooking.
Mama I, too, am interested in gastronomy. I am good cook. Norwegian. I make good Norwegian dishes. Lutefisk. And Kjodboller. That is meatballs with cream sauce.

Mama But she say you are to go on writing. That you have the gift.

Katrin turns back to her, suddenly aglow

And that when you have written story that is real and true . . . then you
send it to someone whose name she give me. (*She fumbles for a piece of
paper*) It is her—agent—and say she recommend you. Here. No,
that is recipe she give me for goulash as her grandmother make it . . .
here. (*She hands over the paper*) It helps, Katrin, what I have told you?
Katrin (*subdued again*) Yes, I—I guess it helps. Some. But what have *I* got
to write about? I haven't seen anything, or been anywhere.
Mama Could you write about San Francisco, maybe? Is fine city. Miss
Moorhead write about her home town.
Katrin Yes, I know. But you've got to have a central character or some-
thing. She writes about her grandfather—he was a wonderful old man.
Mama Could you maybe write about Papa?
Katrin Papa?
Mama Papa is fine man. Is wonderful man.
Katrin Yes, I know, but . . .
Mama (*rising*) I must go fix supper. Is late. Papa will be home. (*She goes up
the steps to the* TABS, *and then turns back*) I like you should write about
Papa.

She exits through the TABS

Katrin (*going back to her seat behind the desk*) Papa. Yes, but what's he
ever done? What's ever happened to him? What's ever happened to *any*
of us? Except always being poor and having illness, like the time when
Dagmar went to hospital and Mama . . . (*The idea hits her like a flash*)
Oh—Oh . . . (*Pause—then she becomes the Katrin of today*) And that was
how it was born—suddenly in a flash—the story of "Mama and the
Hospital"—the first of all the stories. I wrote it—oh, quite soon after
that. I didn't tell Mama or any of them. But I sent it to Miss Moorhead's
agent. It was a long time before I heard anything. And then one evening
the letter came. (*She takes an envelope from the desk in front of her*) For a
moment I couldn't believe it. Then I went rushing into the kitchen,
shouting . . . (*She rises from the desk, taking some papers with her, and
rushes up the steps*) Mama. Mama.

29   *The* TABS *open on the kitchen and the family tableau. Mama is seated* R *of the
table with Christine standing behind her. Papa is seated* L *of the table. Nels
is seated on the chest. Dagmar is not present. Katrin comes rushing in up the
steps. The* R *turntable revolves out as soon as she has left it*

Mama . . . Mama . . . I've sold a story!
Mama A story!
Katrin Yes. I've got a letter from the agent—with a cheque for—(*gasp-
ing*)—five hundred dollars!
Nels No kidding? (*He rises and crosses to* C *above the table*)
Mama Katrin—is true?

Katrin Here it is. Here's the letter. Maybe I haven't read it right. (*She hands the letter to Mama*)

Papa rises and crosses above the table to Mama. They huddle and gloat over the cheque

Christine (*behind Mama's chair*) What will you do with five hundred dollars?
Katrin I don't know. I'll buy Mama her warm coat, I *know* that.
Christine Coats don't cost five hundred dollars.
Katrin I know. We'll put the rest in the bank.
Nels (*kidding*) Quick. Before they change their mind, and stop the cheque.
Katrin Will you, Mama? Will you take it to the bank down-town tomorrow?

Mama looks vague

What is it?
Mama I do not know how.
Nels Just give it to the man and tell him to put it in your account, like you always do.

Mama looks up at Papa

Papa You tell them—now.
Christine Tell us what?
Mama (*desperately*) Is no bank account! (*She rises, feeling hemmed in by them, comes below the table and sits on the bench*) Never in my life have I been inside a bank.
Christine But you always told us . . .
Katrin Mama, you've always said . . .
Mama I know. But was not true. I tell a lie.
Katrin But why, Mama? Why did you pretend?
Mama Is not good for little ones to be afraid . . . to not feel secure. (*Rising and moving* L) But now—with five hundred dollar—I think I can tell.
Katrin (*going to her; emotionally*) Mama!
Mama (*stopping her, quickly*) You read us the story. You have it there?
Katrin Yes.
Mama Then read.
Katrin Now?
Mama Yes. No. Wait. Dagmar must hear. (*She crosses up* R, *opens the pantry door and calls*) Dagmar!
Dagmar (*off*) Yes, Mama.
Mama (*calling*) Come here, I want you!
Dagmar (*off*) What is it?
Mama I want you. No, you leave the rabbits! (*She comes back*) What is it called . . . the story?
Katrin (*sitting in the chair* L *of the table*) It's called "Mama and the Hospital".
Papa (*delighted*) You write about Mama? (*He crosses to the chair below the stove*)
Katrin Yes.

Mama But I thought . . . I thought you say . . . I tell you . . . (*She gestures
at Papa, behind his back*)
Katrin I know, Mama, but—well, that's how it came out.

Dagmar enters up R

Mama sits R *of the table. Papa brings the chair from below the stove, places
it above Mama and sits. Christine sits in the chair* R *above the table and Nels
sits in the chair* L *above the table*

Dagmar What is it? What do you want?
Mama Katrin write story for magazine. They pay her five hundred dollar
to print it.
Dagmar (*completely uninterested*) Oh. (*She starts back for the pantry*)
Mama (*stopping her*) She read it to us. I want you should listen.

Dagmar comes downstage and sits on the floor at Mama's feet

You are ready, Katrin?
Katrin Sure.
Mama Then read.

*The group around the table is now a duplicate of the grouping around Mr
Hyde in the first scene, with Katrin in his place and Christine in Trina's chair*

Katrin (*reading*) "For as long as I could remember, the house on Steiner
Street had been home. All of us were born there. Nels, the oldest and
the only boy . . ."

Nels looks up, astonished to be in a story

". . . my sister, Christine . . ."

Christine looks up

". . . and the littlest sister, Dagmar . . ."
Dagmar Am I in the story?
Mama Hush, Dagmar. We are all in the story.
Katrin "But first and foremost, I remember Mama."

The Lights begin to dim and the CURTAIN *slowly falls*

"I remember that every Saturday night Mama would sit down by the
kitchen table and count out the money Papa had brought home in the
little envelope . . ."

By now, the CURTAIN *is down*

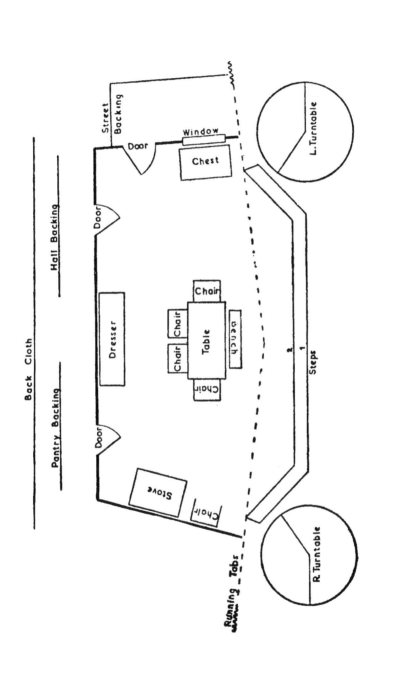

FURNITURE AND PROPERTY LIST

ACT I

1. R. Turntable.
Desk. *On it:* cigarettes, matches, pen, pencil, diary, papers, letter with cheque, manuscript, ashtray
Chair

2. Kitchen
Table. *On it:* envelope and 13 coins, pencil, paper
Dresser. *On it:* small box, 5 cups and saucers, ashtray, workbasket, china as required to dress
Stove. *On it:* coffee pot, spoon.
Chest
On pantry shelf: water jug, milk jug
Off stage R.: cat **(Dagmar)**
Off stage L: box of crayons, scissors, picture book **(Christine)**
Diary **(Katrin)**
Book **(Mr. Hyde)**
Personal: **Papa:** pipe
Christine: handkerchief
Nels: piece of paper, wire puzzle

3. R. Turntable
Desk *as in* 1 *above*

4. L. Turntable
Kitchen table. *On it:* pastry board, rolling pin, dough, raisins, cutter, flour sifter, towel, crochet work

5. Kitchen *as in* 2 *above*
On Table: ashtray
On Chest: doctor's bag and hat
On Dresser: small box
In Car: box of oranges
Off stage L.: blanket **(Dagmar)**
Attaché case **(Mama)**
Personal: **Uncle Chris:** pencil, snuff box

6. R. Turntable
Stepladder.
Pair of roller skates
2 Glasses of milk
2 Plates of biscuits

7. Hospital
   Desk. *On it:* books, papers, pencil, telephone
   Off stage R: mop, pail **(Charwoman)**
   Off stage L: Stethoscope **(Doctor)**
   Tray of dressings **(Orderly)**
   Bag, hat **(Dr. Johnson)**

8. R. Turntable
   Bench
   Chair
   Table. *On it:* potted plant
   On wall: clock

9. Kitchen *as in 2 above*
   Off stage R: apron, bucket, scrubbing brush **(Mama)**

10. L. Turntable
    Bed
    Chair
    Personal: **Uncle Chris:** flask

11. Hospital *as in 7 above*
    In cupboard: mop, bucket.
    Off stage L: charts **(Nurse)**
    Personal: **Katrin:** pencil, paper

ACT II

12. R. Turntable
    Desk *as in 1 above*

13. L. Turntable
    Table. *On it:* sugar basin
    2 Chairs
    Off stage L: cup of coffee, ice-cream soda **(Soda Clerk)**
    Personal: **Mama:** 2 coins, handbag, handkerchief

14. Kitchen *as in 2 above*
    No ashtray on table
    Off stage: R.: tray with bread, butter, milk, jelly **(Mama)**
    Off stage L.: suitcase, letter **(Mr Hyde)**
    School books **(Christine)**
    Books **(Papa)**
    Medicine bottle **(Nels)**
    Personal: **Papa:** newspaper

15. Kitchen *as in 14 above*
    Strike: all books, clothes from chest
    Set—on table: plates, napkins, cups and saucers for five, sugar basin,
    cream jug
    Off stage R.: cat **(Dagmar)**

16. Front Stage
    Off stage R.: school books **(Dagmar)**

17. Kitchen *as in 2 above*
   On table: tray, dishes, sugar basin, 2 cups of coffee
   On Chair below stove: dresser set
   On Chest: Dagmar's hat and coat, Mama's hat and coat
   In Dresser Cupboard: set of draughts and board

18. R. Turntable
   Table with mirror and lights
   Chair

19. Kitchen *as in 2 above*
   On table: sugar basin, cream jug, 2 cups of coffee, coffee pot
   Personal: **Katrin:** brooch in tissue paper

20. L. Turntable
   Table. *On it:* telephone, telephone directory.
   Off stage L.:   piece of toast **(Jenny)**
                    String bag **(Sigrid)**

21. R. Turntable
   Wall telephone
   Telegram

22. Front Stage

23. Bedroom
   Bed
   Table. *On it:* water carafe, glass
   Wash-stand. *On it:* bottle of whisky, water carafe
   Chair
   On Shelf: 3 glasses

24. R. Turntable
   Bench
   Chair
   Personal: **Mama:** notebook, pencil

25. L. Turntable
   Park bench
   Perambulator

26. Kitchen *as in 2 above*
   On Table: workbasket, darning, ashtray, newspaper
   On Chest: book
   Off stage L.:   newspaper, letter **(Nels)**
   Personal: **Nels:** cigarettes, matches

27. L. Turntable
   Couch
   Potted palm
   Personal: **Mama:** Manuscripts, newspaper

28. R. Turntable
   Desk *as in* 1 *above*
   Personal: **Mama:** piece of paper

29. Kitchen *as in 2* above
   On table: darning, ashtray

MADE AND PRINTED IN GREAT BRITAIN BY
LATIMER TREND & COMPANY LTD PLYMOUTH
MADE IN ENGLAND

.